Guardians of the Digital Realm: Navigating Cybersecurity Compliance

Your Essential Guide to Mastering Cyber Regulations at Home and Abroad

by Augustine E. Eta, Ph.D.

Table of Contents

Preface

Get ready to dive into the electrifying world of cybersecurity compliance! Oh yes, this isn't just another dry read filled with jargon that makes your eyes glaze over. No way! Buckle up as we embark on a wild journey that's as much about understanding the invisible threats prowling the digital universe as it is about decoding the labyrinthine regulations that govern them. Why? Because let's face it—the realm of cybersecurity is often as confusing as a maze paved with acronyms, and it can spawn anxiety faster than you can say 'data breach.' In crafting 'Guardians of the Digital Realm,' my goal is to turn those anxieties into power! I'm here to arm you with the confidence, tools, and knowledge necessary to transform compliance from a daunting task into a thrilling adventure. Each chapter has been meticulously designed to guide you from the foundational concepts right up to advanced strategies, meaning every bit of information builds on the last to light your path. But why me? I'm Augustine E. Eta, Ph.D., your friendly Cyber Sentinel, passionate about transforming complex ideas into digestible, relatable nuggets. With a blend of poignant stories, quirky facts, and the wisdom extracted from real-world experiences, we'll put the power back into your hands. This book is a labor of love, inspired by the daily challenges professionals face when navigating the turbulent waters of compliance. I've poured my expertise, research, and practical insights into these pages, hoping to illuminate your understanding of the complex web of cyber threats and the protective regulations designed to combat them. You'll find yourself entranced within the chapters covering everything from understanding the dark alleys of cyber threats to building your very own cyber fortress! The fusion of real-life case studies and vibrant narratives will keep your attention locked in like a steel trap! Expect climactic moments of tension and exhilarating resolutions as we navigate the compliance landscape together! My research spanned countless hours sifting through industry standards and regulations—not the most glamorous task, but one that unveiled the robust frameworks designed to safeguard our digital lives. It was an eye-opening experience! I was determined to create a compendium that not only equips you with essential knowledge but also ignites a fire of empowerment within you. You won't merely skim through; you'll engage, reflect, and ultimately, act! As you traverse through these chapters, I encourage you to absorb the knowledge like a sponge; let these words linger, inspire, and motivate you to advocate for compliance within your organization. This is a shared journey where you become the protagonist in crafting a compliant and secure future. There's a thrill in embarking on this path, and I can't wait for you to discover the empowering insights waiting within. And remember—every page you flip is a step towards mastering the art of cybersecurity compliance. So, arm yourself with a cup of coffee or tea, get comfy, and let's reveal the power of knowledge together until the grand finale! The surprising ending is just the beginning!

With enthusiasm and encouragement,

Augustine E. Eta, Ph.D.

Chapter 1: Unveiling the Threatscape

The Spectrum of Cyber Threats

In the vast and increasingly interconnected digital landscape, the spectrum of cyber threats is as diverse as it is daunting. Organizations and individuals alike find themselves vulnerable to a multitude of cyber dangers, each with unique characteristics, motivations, and consequences. Understanding these threats is the first step in developing effective strategies for protection and compliance.

Cyber threats can be broadly classified into several categories, with each type employing different tactics and targeting various vulnerabilities. From the rudimentary phishing attacks to the sophisticated methodologies employed by advanced persistent threats (APTs), the ways in which attackers exploit systems continue to evolve at an alarming pace.

Phishing attacks, one of the most common forms of cyber threats, epitomize the simplicity with which hackers can deceive unsuspecting individuals. At its core, phishing relies on social engineering techniques to trick victims into revealing sensitive information, such as usernames, passwords, or credit card numbers. Attackers masquerade as trusted entities, often using authentic-looking emails or messages to lure individuals into clicking malicious links or downloading harmful attachments. Common examples include emails supposedly from banks requesting account verification or messages from popular online services alerting users of suspicious activity.

The sheer effectiveness of phishing attacks is alarming. A statistics report indicated that in 2022, nearly 90% of data breaches were facilitated by phishing attempts. Take the notorious case of the 2016 Democratic National Committee email breach, where attackers exploited phishing to gain unauthorized access to sensitive emails. The fallout was immense, exposing vulnerabilities not only within the organization but also impacting public trust in the political process. Such incidents highlight the necessity of continuous training for employees about identifying suspicious correspondence and ensuring robust email security protocols.

Ransomware presents another significant threat on the cyber horizon. Unlike phishing, which seeks to steal information outright, ransomware takes it hostage, demanding a ransom for its release. This type of malware encrypts valuable data within an organization and paralyzes critical systems, often leading to severe operational disruptions. The notorious attack on the city of Baltimore in 2019 serves as a cautionary tale; the city's systems were crippled, resulting in widespread service interruptions and costs exceeding $18 million. This incident illustrates how ransomware can derail operations, driving home the imperative for organizations to adopt stringent data backup strategies and incident response plans.

On the other end of the spectrum lies advanced persistent threats (APTs), which epitomize the sophisticated maneuvering that can occur in cyber warfare. APTs are not merely casual attacks; they are highly organized, long-term operations typically aimed at stealing intellectual property or sensitive information. State-sponsored actors and well-funded cybercriminal organizations often carry out these attacks. A prime example is the SolarWinds attack, where attackers compromised software updates to infiltrate the networks of government agencies and Fortune 500 companies undetected for months. Such breaches not only threaten individual organizations but also national security, demonstrating the far-reaching implications of cyber warfare.

The motivations behind cyber threats are varied, but they primarily fall into three categories: financial gain, ideological or political agendas, and the psychological thrill of the challenge. Financially motivated cybercriminals seek monetary gain through direct theft, extortion, or the trade of stolen information on the dark web. The Equifax data breach of 2017, affecting approximately 147 million Americans, highlights the potential financial consequences of such threats. Attackers exploited vulnerabilities in Equifax's systems and stole sensitive personal data. In its aftermath, the company faced lawsuits, a significant loss of public trust, and a total estimated cost exceeding $4 billion.

Cyber threats driven by ideological motivations often come from hacktivist groups seeking to advance political agendas or social causes. The infamous Anonymous collective is emblematic of this trend, conducting operations against organizations they perceive as unjust or corrupt. Their attacks on the Church of Scientology in 2008, through tactics such as distributed denial-of-service (DDoS) attacks, exemplify the lengths to which such groups will go to voice dissent. These threats challenge organizations not just from a security standpoint but also from an ethical and reputational perspective.

Then there are the thrill-seekers, individuals who conduct cyberattacks out of boredom or a desire to test their skills. While not always resulting in significant damage, their activity can lead to chaos and reputational harm. An illustrative case is the "Teenage Hacker" who, in an effort to impress peers, breached various high-profile corporate websites. Although the financial impact may have been minimal, the disruption and loss of trust could have long-term effects on the affected businesses.

The implications of these different cyber threats can be catastrophic, not only for targeted organizations but for their stakeholders—customers, partners, and even the general public. Each incident represents a breach of trust that reverberates beyond the immediate consequences. Companies considered a safe harbor for sensitive information find that their reputations and future business can suffer collateral damage through just one successful attack.

Beyond the infamous case studies, everyday examples illuminate the pervasive threat of cyber risk. For instance, small businesses often underestimate their vulnerability, believing that since they aren't major corporations, they won't be targeted. Yet, data from cybersecurity firms illustrate that 43% of cyberattacks are aimed at small businesses, with many suffering irreversible losses. The example of a small local café that suffered a ransomware attack illustrates this beautifully. After an attacker encrypted the café's financial records and demanded a ransom, the owner faced an impossible decision: pay the ransom or risk losing everything. Many smaller establishments lack the resources needed to recover from such incidents, often leading to their permanent closure.

As organizations scramble to protect themselves, preventive measures are paramount. Awareness is the first line of defense. Businesses must educate their employees about common scams, instilling a culture of skepticism with respect to unsolicited emails or requests for sensitive information. Regular employee training sessions can demystify phishing attempts, equipping staff with the tools they need to recognize potentially harmful messages.

Moreover, organizations must prioritize the implementation of multi-factor authentication (MFA) across all systems. MFA reinforces security by requiring multiple forms of verification before granting access, even if a password is compromised. Statistics reveal that MFA can block 99.9% of account compromise attacks, showcasing its robust efficacy.

Data encryption should be a standard practice in any organization, protecting sensitive information both at rest and in transit. By employing end-to-end encryption protocols, businesses ensure that even if attackers gain access to data, it remains unintelligible without the encryption key.

Regular software updates and patch management are critical in defending against known vulnerabilities that attackers exploit. Many cyber incidents stem from a lack of timely updates, allowing hackers to enter systems through known weaknesses. Establishing routine maintenance schedules to ensure that systems are kept up to date is essential.

Ultimately, it is essential that businesses adopt a holistic approach to cybersecurity that encompasses technology, people, and processes. By blending technical defenses with cultural awareness and preparedness, organizations can create a formidable barrier against evolving cyber threats.

The cyber threat landscape is a complex and constantly shifting environment that demands vigilance, adaptability, and knowledge. The challenges facing organizations and individuals are significant, but through a proactive stance that emphasizes education and prevention, the worst outcomes can be mitigated. Awareness of the spectrum of cyber threats equips stakeholders to engage with the ever-evolving digital landscape intelligently, fostering resilience in the face of cyber risk.

As the digital realm continues to expand, the importance of remaining aware and informed is paramount. Cyber threats will only become more sophisticated, making it imperative for organizations to stay ahead of disruption through adaptive strategies that shield against known and emerging dangers. By recognizing the multifaceted nature of cyber threats and implementing effective countermeasures, they can truly safeguard their digital assets and ensure compliance in an increasingly chaotic cyber landscape.

The Anatomy of a Cyberattack

The lifecycle of a cyberattack comprises several distinct phases, each critical to understanding how attackers think and operate. By dissecting this process, we can offer organizations the tools necessary for both defense and counterattack. In this subchapter, we will walk through the stages of a cyberattack, from the initial reconnaissance to the aftermath, illuminating how attackers gather intelligence, exploit system vulnerabilities, and maintain persistence within networks. Through real-world examples, we will underscore how even the most secure systems can fall victim to breaches, while also delving into the emotional and strategic challenges IT professionals face during these crises.

Reconnaissance is not merely the first step in an attack; it is arguably the most crucial phase. Attackers conduct reconnaissance to gather information about their intended targets, laying the groundwork for subsequent actions. This stage can be divided into two types: passive and active reconnaissance. Passive reconnaissance involves collecting information without directly interacting with the target. Attackers might scour social media profiles, inspect company websites, or use search engines to identify employee details, technologies in use, and any potential vulnerabilities. This approach allows attackers to form a comprehensive picture of their target while minimizing the risk of detection.

In contrast, active reconnaissance entails direct interaction with the target system. This may include pinging network devices, scanning for open ports, or probing for services that may reveal useful information. Attackers may employ various tools during this phase, such as Nmap or Wireshark, both of which can provide insights into network structure and security controls. A notable example of this step in action occurred in the initial stages of the Target breach in 2013, where attackers scanned the corporate network for vulnerabilities that led to the installation of malware on payment terminals.

After gathering sufficient information, attackers transition to the exploitation phase, where they begin to execute their plans. In this phase, they exploit the vulnerabilities identified during reconnaissance to gain unauthorized access to systems. Common exploitation techniques include exploiting software flaws, employing social engineering tactics, or using malware to deliver their payload. The infamous SolarWinds attack exemplifies this stage well; attackers infiltrated the SolarWinds software supply chain, embedding malware in their updates. As a result, thousands of organizations that updated the software unknowingly introduced a backdoor into their systems.

Once attackers have gained access, the next phase—establishing persistence—becomes vital. It is not enough for attackers to enter a network; they must also ensure they can return whenever they choose. To establish this foothold, attackers often install additional backdoors or modify existing access controls to create infrequent or undetected paths into target networks. A manifestation of this can be seen in the 2016 Democratic National Committee (DNC) breach, where attackers used various methods to maintain prolonged access, allowing them to harvest information over an extended period without detection.

Internal struggles faced by IT professionals surge as the attack escalates. Once a breach is detected—or worse, revealed—IT professionals are thrust into a high-pressure scenario filled with urgency. They face a myriad of challenges, from scrambling to understand the nature and extent of the breach to formulating an immediate plan of action. The urgency is compounded by the need for accurate communication and collaboration across teams, necessitating a clear understanding of roles and responsibilities. Decisions must be made quickly, often informed not by comprehensive data, but by instinctive reactions to safeguard organizational assets.

In the heat of an attack, fear is palpable. IT teams contend not only with the technical aspects of thwarting the attack but also with the emotional toll of potential reputational damage should sensitive data be compromised. For instance, during the Equifax breach in 2017, which exposed the personal information of nearly 147 million people, IT personnel worked tirelessly to manage a crisis that could have profound implications for consumer trust and the organization's future. With each passing hour, the stakes only escalate, forcing professionals to confront the uncomfortable reality that even robust security measures can be breached.

Amid the escalating tensions, IT teams must prioritize containment aimed at limiting damage. This involves isolating affected systems, determining entry points, and analyzing what data might have been exposed. Each decision carries weight, and the consequences of missteps can be dire. Choosing whether to notify customers, stakeholders, or even law enforcement becomes a divisive topic, where timing and messaging can significantly impact public perception and future interactions. Each moment lost might translate into adversarial advantage, further amplifying fears and uncertainties.

The post-attack phase is characterized by recovery and reflection. Once the immediate threat is contained and remedial steps are taken, organizations must pivot to understanding what transpired. This retrospective analysis is paramount, as it reveals the weaknesses that allowed the attack to succeed and will inform future cybersecurity strategies. An effective post-attack assessment entails thorough documentation of the incident, discussions about what went wrong, and identification of missed warning signs.

Afterward, organizations can draft a comprehensive incident report, generally including timelines of the breach, actions taken, and lessons learned. Real-world examples provide insight into the importance of this phase; the aftermath of the Yahoo breaches emphasized the necessity of improved security protocols. The multimillion-dollar penalties levied on Yahoo—a consequence of their slow response and lack of transparency—illustrate the critical nature of reflection post-incident. Companies that take the time to assess their shortcomings and implement corrective measures not only enhance security but also build resilience against future threats.

Moreover, this reflective exercise leads organizations to re-evaluate their compliance frameworks. As regulatory scrutiny grows, understanding the cybersecurity anatomy becomes crucial for organizations trying to navigate increasingly complex legal landscapes. Using insights gained from previous incidents can enhance the robustness of compliance strategies, ensuring that the organization meets necessary regulatory standards and builds consumer trust.

Finally, the attack lifecycle is not linear; organizations must sustain vigilance to protect their defenses against potential future breaches. Attackers continue to evolve, leveraging new technologies and tactics. For instance, with the growing prevalence of IoT devices, an entirely new realm of vulnerabilities emerges, necessitating continuous training and updates to compliance measures. Understanding the anatomy of existing threats allows IT teams to anticipate and mitigate against future attacks, thus evolving alongside aggressive adversaries.

As organizations prepare for an uncertain future, instilling a culture of cybersecurity resilience becomes essential. This is accomplished through ongoing training, simulated phishing attacks, and workshops designed to recognize suspicious behavior and engage in proactive cybersecurity practices. Successful navigation of this landscape not only prepares organizations for the possibility of an attack but instills the notion that compliance and resilience are indeed allies, not merely goals to be checked off during audits.

Ultimately, the anatomy of a cyberattack serves as a crucial map for organizations to comprehend the motivations, methodologies, and implications of the adversarial landscape. By dissecting the lifecycle into identifiable stages—from reconnaissance to post-attack analysis—organizations can equip themselves with knowledge vital for effective response and recovery planning. This comprehensive understanding fosters resilience, enabling businesses to not only defend sensitive data but also cultivate an agile operation that thrives amid threat-filled waters.

By learning from real-world precedents and the internal struggles faced by IT professionals during an attack, organizations can establish frameworks that allow for agility and proactive behaviors. Strong leadership in cybersecurity drives cultural change, reinforcing that every member of the organization has a role in protecting data. As the digital landscape continues to morph, it is crucial that organizations remain vigilant, understanding not only their vulnerabilities but also the mechanisms available to thwart potential attacks.

In a world increasingly fraught with cyber threats, a thorough understanding of the anatomy of cyberattacks is of paramount importance. Organizations must prepare to respond with methodical precision to deter threats and recover effectively should they occur. Thus, the challenge remains: to transform knowledge into action and maintain an unwavering commitment to cybersecurity compliance that evolves in tandem with the disruption of digital innovation. By turning the insights gained from dissecting the attack lifecycle into action items, organizations stand a stronger chance of navigating today's perilous digital threatscape.

The Impact of Cyber Threats on Society

Cyber threats have seeped beyond the confines of individual organizations, seizing entire sectors and communities, redefining our interconnected existence. The repercussions of these attacks extend far beyond mere monetary losses; they resonate at the very core of societal trust, economic stability, and national security. A breach at a hospital can result in more than personal data theft—it can lead to hindered medical services, potentially putting lives at risk. A cyber intrusion at a government agency can compromise sensitive information, threatening national security and, by extension, the safety of citizens.

Consider the well-documented data breaches that have gripped companies like Equifax, Target, and Yahoo. Each breach shook consumer confidence, revealing the fragility of the data-mediated world we inhabit. For instance, in 2017, a breach at Equifax exposed the personal information of approximately 147 million individuals, leading to an erosion of trust not just in that credit reporting agency but across the entire financial sector. Consumers, once trusting of such institutions to safeguard their sensitive information, became skeptical, often opting for minimal interactions or hostile decisions, such as freezing their credit lines. The implications of this extend far beyond the breach itself, amplifying the uncertainty surrounding data protection in financial dealings.

The economic ramifications of cyber threats are manifold. Businesses that experience data breaches incur direct costs, including legal fees, investigation expenses, and penalties assessed by regulatory agencies. In addition to tangible financial burdens, the companies also suffer from reputational damage, leading to a loss of customers and, ultimately, revenue. Research from the Ponemon Institute indicates that the average cost of a data breach in the United States exceeded $8 million in 2022, reflecting an upward trajectory. However, the broader economy also feels the sting, as economic instability can languish in the shadows of such incidents. When consumers distrust the systems that underpin their daily lives, they become less likely to engage in the economy, stunting growth and innovation.

The psychological toll of cybercrime cannot be overlooked. Victims often report feelings of anxiety, shame, and vulnerability after a breach. A powerful illustration of this can be drawn from the experiences of a small business owner whose organization suffered a ransomware attack. Faced with demands for bitcoin to regain access to their critical operating systems, the owner was not only plunged into a financial crisis but also burdened by the emotional weight of fear and helplessness. The aftermath of such an event often necessitates significant spending on cybersecurity improvements and, in many cases, compromises the business's ability to serve its customers effectively. The incident served as a visceral reminder of the disconnect between the digital and emotional realms within communities.

Consider the victim of identity theft, who finds their life upended by a hacker using their personal information to secure loans, open credit cards, and wreak general havoc. In telling their story, Jane, a 32-year-old marketing professional, recounted her experience after her identity was stolen. “I felt like I was living in a nightmare; it was as if I had become invisible. My credit score plummeted overnight, and I spent countless hours contacting creditors, clearing my name. It changes you. You start second-guessing every online action.” The emotional toll manifests not just as personal anguish but also as a societal issue, contributing to increased mental health challenges across broader populations.

The societal fabric, too, witnesses a gradual unraveling stemming from cyber threats. With malicious actors leveraging data to further their agendas, public confidence in institutions wanes. Scandals rooted in betrayal of trust can lead to political upheaval, as citizens begin questioning the integrity of their leaders and the systems of governance. The intersection of cybercrime and politics is exemplified in the exploitation of social media platforms to manipulate public opinion, shape electoral outcomes, or incite discord. The Cambridge Analytica scandal serves as a poignant reminder of how sensitive data can be weaponized to foster division, eroding the very foundations of a democratic society.

In light of these evolving threats, ethical considerations come to the forefront. Corporations, often driven by profit and shareholder value, face the critical dilemma of balancing business objectives with their responsibilities to protect consumer data. “The tension between compliance and ethics is an ongoing struggle,” shares Linda, a corporate ethics officer. “On one hand, we’re driven by the need to innovate and expand; on the other hand, we have a duty to safeguard our customers. The two aren't always compatible." Information security is not merely an IT issue; it has become an existential question for organizations tasked with preserving both consumer confidence and operational viability.

Customers today require more than just assurances that their data is safe; they demand transparency and accountability from the businesses they choose to engage with. Following a data breach, organizations are frequently called upon to not only resolve the immediate crisis but also engage in open dialogue with those affected, elucidating the steps they have taken to remediate the breach and prevent its recurrence. Establishing trust requires a commitment to long-term investment in cybersecurity, standing against adversaries employing increasingly sophisticated methods to acquire sensitive data.

One crucial area where ethical considerations intersect with cybersecurity compliance is in the treatment of personal data. Striking a balance between data monetization and privacy rights is a hot-button issue in today's digital market, where personal information is frequently viewed as an asset. The General Data Protection Regulation (GDPR) was implemented in the European Union as an effort to enhance consumer protection and impose tough fines on organizations that fail to comply. Its reach sets a global standard, yet many companies remain out of step, continuing to place profit over people.

The ethical ramifications of these choices reverberate through society. For the modern consumer, understanding how their data is used—or misused—creates an ethical imperative for businesses to act responsibly. A story from Maxine, a data analyst with a local tech startup, underscores this point. “We faced backlash from customers when they discovered that our data policies were lax. It wasn’t just about lost customers; it disrupted our whole morale as a team. We had to face the music and take genuine steps to reestablish trust, searching for more ethical avenues for data use. It was a tough, but necessary lesson.”

Businesses must confront the societal implications of their cybersecurity practices. The dialogue surrounding data security is evolving, with informed consumers holding organizations accountable for ethical breaches. Failures in data protection don’t just result in isolated incidents; they contribute to a broader atmosphere of fear and distrust within society. Cybersecurity is now more than a compliance checklist; it represents a commitment to societal well-being.

As society leans increasingly on technology, the implications of cyber threats can no longer be contained within organizational boundaries; they spill into the public arena, challenging notions of governance, accountability, and ethics. To address the multifaceted dimensions of this issue, it is essential to foster a holistic understanding of the stakes involved and the impact these threats have on communities at large.

Emerging from these discussions is the recognition that data breaches catalyze societal change, compelling individuals, businesses, and governments to reassess their approaches to data security and personal accountability. The incremental realization that cybersecurity is a shared responsibility ignites a movement for greater awareness and proactive engagement. By intertwining ethical considerations with the lived experiences of victims, the narrative around cyber threats becomes a rallying cry for enriched consumer protections and greater accountability among corporations.

Final thoughts echo the sentiment that the future of cybersecurity demands a collective effort. It is imperative that individuals, organizations, and governments unite in the fight against cyber threats, forging a path that prioritizes accountability, safeguards consumer trust, and champions ethical practices. While the ramifications of cybercrime may appear daunting, the potential for learning and growth remains. In the face of adversity, there exists an opportunity for society to emerge more vigilant, more informed, and, ultimately, more resilient in the battle against cyber threats.

The journey toward a safer digital landscape will require participating in this dialogue, championing the protection of personal data, and creating a culture in which cybersecurity is seen not as a burden but as a shared ethical obligation. Together, we can mitigate the impacts of cyber threats on society and safeguard the trust that forms the bedrock of our interconnected world. As we move forward, the impetus remains to transform the fear instilled by cybercrime into an unwavering commitment to protect each other and our collective future.

Chapter 2: Guardrails of Governance

Understanding Cybersecurity Regulations

In an era defined by the rapid digitization of information, the importance of cybersecurity regulations cannot be overstated. Organizations around the globe are faced with the daunting task of safeguarding sensitive data, making compliance with relevant regulations imperative for operational integrity and consumer trust. This subchapter will illuminate the key cybersecurity regulations that businesses must navigate, including the General Data Protection Regulation (GDPR), the Health Insurance Portability and Accountability Act (HIPAA), and the Payment Card Industry Data Security Standard (PCI DSS). Through engaging narratives and illustrative case studies, readers will gain a nuanced understanding of these regulations, the challenges of compliance, and the far-reaching consequences of non-compliance.

The General Data Protection Regulation (GDPR)

The GDPR, established in April 2016 and fully enforced by May 2018, represents a landmark evolution in data protection legislation within the European Union (EU). Its primary objective is to enhance individuals' control over their personal data and to streamline data privacy regulations across Europe. Originating from the need for a comprehensive framework applicable to all member states, the GDPR has reshaped how organizations handle personal data.

At its core, the GDPR mandates that organizations must process personal data lawfully, transparently, and for specified legitimate purposes. Key provisions include the rights of individuals to access their data, the right to rectification, the right to erasure (commonly known as the "right to be forgotten"), and the right to data portability. Additionally, organizations are required to conduct Data Protection Impact Assessments (DPIAs) when initiating processes likely to result in high risks to the rights and freedoms of individuals.

The implications of GDPR compliance extend well beyond the EU's borders. Organizations worldwide that handle the personal data of EU citizens must comply with its stringent requirements or risk facing hefty fines. The substantial monetary penalties—up to 4% of global annual turnover or €20 million, whichever is higher—underscore the law's strict enforcement mechanisms.

One notable case illustrating the challenges of GDPR compliance occurred with British Airways in 2019. Following a significant data breach, the airline faced an unprecedented fine of £183 million for failing to adequately protect customer data. The breach exposed personal information of roughly 500,000 customers, prompting the Information Commissioner's Office (ICO) to conduct an investigation. This incident not only highlighted the financial repercussions of non-compliance but also underscored the critical importance of robust data protection measures within organizations.

Navigating GDPR compliance can be intricate, particularly for businesses that operate across multiple jurisdictions. Organizations must engage in thorough data audits to inventory the types of personal data they collect, establish clear privacy policies, and implement mechanisms for obtaining valid consent from individuals. Furthermore, they must cultivate a culture of data protection within their workforce through ongoing training and awareness programs.

The Health Insurance Portability and Accountability Act (HIPAA)

HIPAA, enacted in 1996, is a cornerstone of healthcare data regulation in the United States. Designed to safeguard the privacy and security of individuals' health information, HIPAA sets forth a comprehensive framework for the protection of sensitive patient data throughout the healthcare sector.

One of the key components of HIPAA is the Privacy Rule, which establishes national standards for the protection of certain health information, known as Protected Health Information (PHI). The Privacy Rule gives individuals the right to receive and access their health information, as well as the right to request corrections to their medical records. It also restricts covered entities—healthcare providers, health plans, and healthcare clearinghouses—from sharing PHI without patient consent, except for specific circumstances such as treatment, payment, and healthcare operations.

In addition to the Privacy Rule, HIPAA enforces the Security Rule, which mandates that covered entities and their business associates implement administrative, physical, and technical safeguards to protect electronic Protected Health Information (ePHI). These safeguards include access control measures, encryption, and regular risk assessments.

The importance of HIPAA compliance is highlighted by the consequences of failure to meet its provisions. One illustrative case involved Anthem Inc., a major health insurance provider that suffered a data breach in 2015, resulting in the exposure of approximately 78.8 million individuals' PHI. Subsequently, Anthem was fined $16 million by the Department of Health and Human Services (HHS) for failing to implement adequate security measures and for not conducting a thorough risk analysis that could have prevented the breach. This case exemplifies the financial and reputational toll of non-compliance while emphasizing the necessity of proactive risk management practices within healthcare organizations.

Organizations subject to HIPAA regulations must continually assess their compliance posture, ensuring that protocols for safeguarding patient information are effectively designed and enforced. This includes conducting regular staff training to raise awareness of HIPAA requirements and best practices for data protection and security. Moreover, healthcare organizations must establish comprehensive incident response protocols, ensuring they are equipped to mitigate the impact of potential data breaches swiftly and effectively.

The Payment Card Industry Data Security Standard (PCI DSS)

In the wake of increasing data breaches related to payment card information, the Payment Card Industry Security Standards Council (PCI SSC) introduced the PCI DSS in 2004. This regulation sets forth a robust framework aimed at protecting cardholder data and ensuring secure payment transactions across organizations that process credit and debit card information.

PCI DSS encompasses a series of security requirements divided into twelve key areas, which include building and maintaining a secure network, protecting cardholder data, implementing strong access control measures, regularly monitoring and testing networks, and maintaining an information security policy. Compliance with these standards is mandatory for all entities that accept credit cards, ranging from small businesses to large enterprises.

The ramifications of non-compliance can be severe, as evidenced by the 2013 Target data breach, wherein hackers accessed credit card information of approximately 40 million customers. Target was subsequently fined $18.5 million in a multi-state settlement and faced additional penalties from credit card companies. This breach underscored the importance of PCI compliance, demonstrating how inadequate security measures can lead to dire financial consequences and long-lasting damage to customer trust.

As organizations work to achieve compliance with PCI DSS, they must establish comprehensive data protection strategies, incorporating regular vulnerability scans, penetration testing, and security awareness training for employees. Moreover, organizations must engage in continuous monitoring of their payment systems, ensuring they remain vigilant against evolving cyber threats and consistently adhere to regulatory requirements.

Consequences of Non-Compliance

The consequences of non-compliance with cybersecurity regulations can be profound and multifaceted, impacting not only an organization's financial stability but also its reputation, customer trust, and operational continuity. Regulatory bodies are increasingly vigilant in their enforcement efforts, and organizations failing to meet compliance requirements may face hefty fines, legal actions, and damaging public scrutiny.

Real-world case studies serve to illustrate the potentially catastrophic results of non-compliance. In addition to the previously mentioned cases of British Airways, Anthem, and Target, another salient example is that of Equifax, the credit reporting agency that suffered a massive data breach in 2017, exposing the personal data of approximately 147 million people. Equifax faced severe backlash and was ultimately hit with a $700 million settlement due to violations of the Fair Credit Reporting Act, among other charges. This incident demonstrated how failing to address vulnerabilities can lead to significant breaches, raising questions about the organization's commitment to data protection.

The financial impact of non-compliance extends beyond immediate fines. Organizations may also experience increased liability related to customer lawsuits and settlements stemming from data breaches. Following incidents of non-compliance, organizations often struggle with diminished consumer confidence and loyalty, which can further erode revenues. The ripple effects can be felt not only by the companies themselves but also throughout their supply chains and among industry competitors.

Moreover, the reputation damage from non-compliance can lead to long-term challenges, diminishing stakeholder trust, and impacting relationships with customers and partners. A negative perception in the marketplace may hinder future business opportunities, making organizations less competitive within their respective industries.

In contrast, organizations that prioritize cybersecurity compliance often reap significant benefits, including enhanced operational efficiency, improved security posture, and a competitive advantage in an increasingly security-conscious marketplace. By embracing compliance as a core organizational value rather than a mere obligation, these organizations foster resilience in the face of cyber threats and success in their regulatory endeavors.

Navigating the Complex Landscape of Cybersecurity Regulations

For organizations striving to remain compliant with cybersecurity regulations, navigating this complex landscape can prove to be a daunting task. The convergence of varying regulatory requirements, organizational cultures, and technological advancements necessitates a strategic approach to compliance.

To begin with, organizations must invest in a thorough understanding of the regulatory frameworks that apply to their specific industries. This often entails conducting comprehensive risk assessments to identify areas of vulnerability and develop robust policies and procedures tailored to distinct compliance requirements. Additionally, organizations should establish dedicated compliance teams responsible for monitoring changes in regulations, as well as overseeing the implementation of compliance initiatives.

Furthermore, fostering an organizational culture that prioritizes data privacy and security is crucial for effective compliance. Employee training programs designed to educate staff on regulatory requirements and best practices can enhance overall organizational awareness and promote a culture of accountability. Engaging in regular audits and assessments is also essential for verifying adherence to compliance standards and identifying potential gaps that may warrant corrective action.

In conclusion, understanding cybersecurity regulations such as GDPR, HIPAA, and PCI DSS is essential for organizations operating in today's digital landscape. The repercussions of non-compliance can be severe, impacting not only an organization's financial bottom line but also its reputation and stakeholder trust. By prioritizing compliance as a strategic imperative, organizations can position themselves to not only meet regulatory mandates but also effectively protect their sensitive data and safeguard against the evolving landscape of cyber threats. This commitment to cybersecurity governance serves as a foundational pillar for building resilience in the face of uncertainty and fostering trust within the organizations they serve.

Frameworks for Cybersecurity Governance

In today's digital landscape, where threats to cybersecurity are continuously evolving, organizations must adopt effective governance frameworks that offer structured guidance for managing cybersecurity risks. The significance of these frameworks transcends mere compliance; they serve as blueprints that strategically direct organizations in safeguarding their assets, ensuring resilience in the face of cyber threats. In this subchapter, we will delve into some of the most prominent cybersecurity frameworks, including NIST Cybersecurity Framework, ISO/IEC 27001, and COBIT, exploring their unique structures, applications, and advantages. We will also emphasize the critical importance of selecting the right framework based on an organization's specific needs and objectives.

The NIST Cybersecurity Framework, developed by the National Institute of Standards and Technology, represents one of the most comprehensive approaches to cybersecurity governance. Its development was spurred by a directive from the Executive Order on Improving Critical Infrastructure Cybersecurity in 2013, which aimed to provide a voluntary framework for reducing cybersecurity risks. The framework comprises five core functions: Identify, Protect, Detect, Respond, and Recover.

The Identify function focuses on understanding the organization's environment and the critical infrastructure that supports its operations. This entails asset management, risk assessment, and governance structure—elements fundamental to establishing a solid cybersecurity foundation. With an effective identification process, organizations can discern their vulnerabilities and prioritize their cybersecurity efforts accordingly.

The Protect function encompasses the measures organizations put in place to safeguard their critical assets. This includes implementing security policies, access control measures, and training staff on cybersecurity best practices.

Emphasizing protective measures is paramount as it helps mitigate risks before they evolve into actual breaches.

The Detect function involves continuous monitoring for potential cybersecurity incidents. It encourages organizations to establish capabilities for continuous detection of anomalies and security events, thereby enabling them to identify breaches before significant damage occurs. This proactive approach is crucial for maintaining an organization's defensive posture.

Once a potential breach is detected, the Respond function comes into play. This aspect of the framework outlines the procedures and capabilities required to respond to cybersecurity incidents effectively. A well-defined response plan ensures organizations can quickly mitigate the impact of a breach and restore normal operations.

Finally, the Recover function focuses on the organization's ability to restore services following a cybersecurity incident. This includes developing strategic recovery plans to enhance resilience and reduce recovery time and costs.

The NIST Cybersecurity Framework is not just about compliance; it is about establishing a resilient cybersecurity culture within an organization. Its flexible structure allows organizations, regardless of their size or sector, to tailor the framework to their unique requirements. This adaptability is one of its greatest strengths, fostering ongoing evolution and improvement in cybersecurity efforts.

In our discussions with industry experts regarding the NIST framework, many emphasized its significance as a risk management-oriented approach. "Rather than seeing cybersecurity as a checkbox exercise," one cybersecurity consultant noted, "organizations should view the NIST framework as an ongoing commitment to understanding and reducing risk."

Similarly, another security officer conveyed, "The comprehensive structure of NIST allows organizations to communicate about cyber risks in a common language, bridging the gap between technical teams and business leadership. This alignment is vital for effective governance."

In contrast, ISO/IEC 27001, an international standard for Information Security Management Systems (ISMS), provides a systematic approach to managing sensitive information. Developed by the International Organization for Standardization (ISO), this framework specifies a set of requirements for establishing, implementing, maintaining, and continually improving an ISMS.

Organizations adopting ISO 27001 benefit from its clearly defined requirements, which emphasize the importance of establishing a robust risk management process. The risk assessment and treatment process requires organizations to assess their information security risks, identify vulnerabilities, and apply adequate controls to mitigate these risks. Importantly, ISO 27001 allows organizations to prioritize security measures based on risk levels, aligning security investments with their business objectives.

One of the defining aspects of ISO 27001 is its strong focus on continual improvement. This process ensures that organizations regularly assess the effectiveness of their ISMS and adapt to new threats or changes in the business environment. The framework promotes a culture of continuous improvement, fostering an organization-wide commitment to information security.

Furthermore, the certification process associated with ISO 27001 can also provide organizations with significant advantages. Achieving certification demonstrates a commitment to information security management, instilling confidence in customers, partners, and stakeholders. It positions organizations as responsible stewards of sensitive data, which is increasingly important in today's data-driven landscape.

In conversations with compliance officers and information security managers, the growing importance of ISO 27001 as a competitive differentiator was another theme that emerged. “More clients are demanding assurances that their data will be handled securely,” remarked a chief compliance officer at a multinational corporation. “Achieving ISO 27001 certification not only helps meet this expectation but also strengthens our brand.”

Meanwhile, COBIT, originally developed by ISACA, offers an alternative approach focusing on the governance and management of enterprise IT. Whereas the NIST framework and ISO 27001 are primarily centered on cybersecurity and information security, respectively, COBIT provides a broader governance framework that encompasses the entirety of IT management and control.

The latest iteration, COBIT 2019, includes updated components designed to enhance its relevance in today’s dynamic business environment. It comprises governance and management objectives, governance system and components, performance management, and a design guide to support effective governance structures.

One of COBIT's core values lies in its emphasis on aligning IT goals with business objectives. This strategic alignment underscores the importance of governance efforts rooted in an organization's overarching goals and vision. Organizations adopting COBIT can develop a tailored governance system that addresses specific business challenges, ensuring that information and technology contribute meaningfully to business success.

As organizations navigate the complexities of compliance, selecting the appropriate framework can be a critical endeavor. The choice ultimately should be influenced by various factors, including organizational size, industry, regulatory requirements, and specific organizational goals. For instance, a healthcare organization might prioritize compliance with HIPAA regulations and therefore may find the NIST framework particularly suitable for its risk-based approach. Meanwhile, a technology startup aiming for international collaboration might prioritize ISO 27001 certification to instill confidence in global partners.

Through conversations with cybersecurity consultants and governance experts, the strategic importance of assessing organizational needs before framework selection was emphasized repeatedly. "It's not a one-size-fits-all approach," one expert elaborated. "Different organizations face unique threats and have distinct compliance requirements, so their choice of framework should reflect that."

Moreover, organizations can also choose to integrate elements from multiple frameworks to create a tailored governance approach. This hybrid approach allows organizations to leverage the strengths of multiple frameworks, addressing specific compliance needs while ensuring a comprehensive governance structure.

To successfully implement these frameworks, organizations must adopt best practices for organizational engagement, resource allocation, and training. Critical to this success is fostering a collaboration between IT and non-IT departments. Various cybersecurity frameworks emphasize the need for a unified approach to bear the responsibility of cybersecurity across the organization. Involving all relevant stakeholders increases awareness of cybersecurity issues and enhances organizational resilience.

Additionally, investing in training and education for employees at all levels is paramount. Ensuring that staff members understand the principles behind the chosen framework fosters a proactive cybersecurity culture. According to one cybersecurity educator, “When everyone in the organization understands their role in cybersecurity, the collective power of that awareness serves as the first line of defense.”

Another best practice is to establish metrics for measuring compliance effectiveness. Each of the frameworks discussed—NIST, ISO 27001, and COBIT—provides guidance on defining key performance indicators (KPIs) that can help organizations gauge their progress. By regularly assessing their compliance status and making necessary adjustments, organizations can support continuous improvement in governance efforts.

While the frameworks we have discussed provide robust guidance for cybersecurity governance, organizations must now consider how they will adapt to dynamically evolving technological landscapes. As new technologies, such as artificial intelligence, machine learning, and cloud computing, continue to shape the business environment, traditional cybersecurity frameworks must also evolve.

Experts in the field highlight the importance of keeping abreast of emerging trends to ensure that governance frameworks remain relevant and effective. “Lack of adaptability leads not only to compliance failures but also to missed opportunities for innovation,” argues a prominent cybersecurity strategist. “Organizations should continually evaluate their frameworks against new threats and corporate strategies.”

Overall, the implementation of cybersecurity frameworks like NIST, ISO 27001, and COBIT provides organizations with a roadmap for building effective cybersecurity governance structures. The choice of framework should resonate with the organization’s specific needs while allowing for customization based on a thorough understanding of inherent risks.

As organizations increasingly recognize the importance of strong governance frameworks, they will be better positioned to safeguard their sensitive data and ensure longevity in the ever-evolving digital landscape. A well-implemented framework not only enhances regulatory compliance but also fosters resilience and establishes an organizational culture committed to cybersecurity. As the cybersecurity landscape continues to evolve, frameworks will remain critical in navigating the complexities of governance, compliance, and risk management. Organizations that effectively leverage these frameworks will not only protect their assets but also position themselves as trusted leaders in cybersecurity governance, ultimately fortifying their relevance in the digital realm.

Building a Culture of Compliance

In the world of cybersecurity, the importance of compliance extends far beyond mere adherence to regulations. It encompasses the very heart of an organization: its people. A culture of compliance rooted in cybersecurity awareness and accountability not only protects sensitive data but also fosters trust and integrity. This subchapter will explore how organizations can cultivate this essential culture among employees, emphasizing the role of leadership, effective training programs, and real-world examples of success.

At its core, building a culture of compliance means instilling a mindset that values security in every aspect of business operations. A successful culture is one where every employee understands their role in safeguarding the organization, and where compliance is viewed not as a burdensome obligation, but as an integral part of the company's mission. This shift in perspective is crucial, especially in a landscape where cyber threats are increasingly sophisticated and pervasive.

Leadership plays an instrumental role in shaping this culture. When executives prioritize cybersecurity and compliance, they set the tone for the entire organization. They must demonstrate their commitment through actions that resonate with employees, whether it be participating in training sessions, speaking openly about the importance of cybersecurity, or allocating resources toward compliance initiatives. Such involvement can effectively bridge the gap between compliance policies and daily practices, encouraging employees to actively engage in and take ownership of their roles within the cybersecurity framework.

One real-world example of strong leadership promoting a culture of compliance can be seen with a multinational retailer that faced a high-profile data breach. Following the incident, their executive team made the strategic decision to prioritize cybersecurity culture throughout the organization. They began by implementing comprehensive training programs designed to educate all employees about the evolving landscape of cyber threats. These training sessions were not mere check-the-box exercises; they emphasized storytelling and real-life scenarios that resonated with employees, making the content relatable and impactful. The leadership team made it clear that cyber hygiene was the shared responsibility of everyone, from the warehouse staff to top executives. To further reinforce this culture, they instituted regular "Cybersecurity Awareness Weeks," featuring workshops, guest speakers, and interactive sessions that encouraged collaboration across departments.

In addition to leadership visibility, training programs must be developed with relevance and engagement in mind. As overwhelming as compliance regulations can be, organizations can foster a culture of awareness by designing training materials that are both educational and entertaining. This includes incorporating gamified elements into training sessions where employees can compete in quizzes that test their knowledge of cybersecurity best practices. Not only does gamification make learning more enjoyable, but it also promotes retention of critical information and encourages healthy competition among teams.

An eye-opening case study involves a financial institution that successfully transformed its culture through innovative training. Recognizing that their employees were frequently the weakest link in the security chain, the organization implemented a year-long program called "Securing Our Future." This initiative involved monthly thematic campaigns focusing on different aspects of cybersecurity, such as phishing awareness, data privacy best practices, and protecting personal devices. Each theme was accompanied by interactive learning modules, peer-led discussions, and informative newsletters that highlighted real-life breaches and their consequences. The program culminated in an annual Cyber Awareness Day where employees were honored for outstanding participation and contributions, further reinforcing the importance of cybersecurity within their roles.

Moreover, fostering a culture of compliance requires the establishment of clear communication channels. Organizations must ensure that employees feel comfortable reporting potential security incidents or suggesting improvements to processes without fear of repercussions. This can be achieved by developing a transparent reporting system that emphasizes confidentiality and creates a sense of community. For instance, creating an anonymous feedback mechanism can facilitate an open dialogue where employees can voice concerns or ask questions about compliance practices.

Recognizing and rewarding positive behaviors associated with compliance is another effective strategy for instilling a culture of accountability. For example, implementing a recognition program that celebrates employees who exemplify best practices in cybersecurity can motivate others to follow their lead. This might involve highlighting employee initiatives that enhance security measures or showcasing proactive actions taken to prevent data breaches. By framing compliance not just as a requirement, but as a valued contribution, organizations can strengthen the collective commitment to cybersecurity.

It is also essential to recognize that a culture of compliance is not a one-time initiative but rather an ongoing process. Organizations should regularly reassess their compliance culture and adapt training and policies as necessary. Conducting periodic audits, employee surveys, and focus groups can provide insights into areas where the organization excels and where improvements are needed. This longitudinal approach signals to employees that their input is valued and that leadership is committed to continuous improvement in cybersecurity posture.

As organizations work to build this culture of compliance, they must also navigate the challenges that may arise. Employees may feel overwhelmed by the sheer volume of information presented in training sessions or resist new policies perceived as infringing on their autonomy. To address these concerns, leaders must communicate the rationale behind compliance efforts clearly. An explanation of how proper cybersecurity practices protect not just the company but also employees' personal information can foster buy-in and understanding. Additionally, organizations can seek to personalize approaches by tailoring training to fit various roles and departments within the organization. This enables employees to understand how compliance directly impacts their specific positions, leading to greater engagement.

Further reinforcing the role of leadership, organizations should encourage executives to actively engage in and promote compliance initiatives. This can be done by appointing executive sponsors for various compliance training programs, thereby giving them a stake in the success of the initiative. Such sponsorship can be instrumental in enhancing the visibility of compliance efforts while ensuring that resources and support are allocated appropriately.

A notable example of this approach can be seen in a major healthcare provider that faced rapid regulatory changes due to new data protection requirements. The CEO and other top executives took the initiative to lead the development of a comprehensive compliance strategy while ensuring that various department heads were involved in the implementation process. These leaders not only participated in training sessions but also led workshops within their departments, encouraging an open discussion about compliance challenges and best practices. By embedding compliance at every level of the organization, they successfully created an environment where employees recognized their contributions to a culture of cybersecurity and felt a sense of ownership in safeguarding sensitive patient information.

Lastly, organizations should never underestimate the value of external partnerships and collaborations in fostering a compliance culture. Many organizations can benefit from partnerships with educational institutions, industry experts, or cybersecurity consultants to develop robust training programs. Leverage these partnerships to deliver fresh perspectives on training and help establish connections with other professionals who share common compliance objectives. Furthermore, involving external speakers for workshops and seminars can inspire employees and provide real-world insights into the importance of compliance, especially when those speakers share experiences from their backgrounds.

Ultimately, building a culture of compliance centered on cybersecurity awareness and accountability is a multifaceted endeavor. Organizations must embrace the human aspect of compliance—the true security resides not just within policies and tools, but within the collective mindset of employees. Through strong leadership commitment, engaging training programs, clear communication, recognition of positive behaviors, and ongoing evaluation, organizations can cultivate a sustainable compliance culture that transforms cybersecurity from a mere obligation into a fundamental aspect of their identity.

As we move further into this digital age, the need for a resilient culture of compliance has never been more critical. Organizations that prioritize this will not only enhance their cybersecurity posture but will also build stronger relationships with customers, stakeholders, and the community at large. Subsequently, they will emerge as leaders in the digital realm, demonstrating that cybersecurity compliance is not merely a checkbox activity but a core value that can empower the "Guardians of the Digital Realm."

Chapter 3: Cybersecurity Standards Decoded

Deciphering Industry Standards

In the rapidly evolving landscape of cybersecurity, the multitude of industry standards can seem overwhelming. However, understanding these guidelines is crucial for organizations trying to navigate compliance requirements and mitigate the risks associated with cyber threats. Industry standards serve as benchmarks for establishing robust cybersecurity practices, ensuring that organizations can effectively protect sensitive data and maintain customer trust. This subchapter aims to elucidate the various industry standards that guide cybersecurity compliance, comparing them side by side and examining their specific frameworks to facilitate best practices.

Let's begin with the foundational standards that have become pillars in the cybersecurity field: the NIST Cybersecurity Framework, ISO/IEC 27001, and the Payment Card Industry Data Security Standard (PCI DSS). Though each standard serves distinct purposes, they intersect in their objectives to enhance information security and foster resilience against cyber risks.

The NIST Cybersecurity Framework, developed by the National Institute of Standards and Technology, provides a comprehensive set of guidelines for managing cybersecurity risk based on existing standards and best practices. It is divided into five core functions: Identify, Protect, Detect,

Respond, and Recover. By adopting the NIST Framework, organizations are encouraged to assess their current cybersecurity practices, identify potential vulnerabilities, develop strategies for protection, and establish protocols for detection and response to incidents.

For instance, the case of a mid-sized financial institution illustrates the framework's effectiveness. Faced with increasing cyber threats, the organization conducted a risk assessment using the NIST Framework, which helped identify gaps in its security posture. By following the guidelines, they strengthened their incident response capabilities and achieved a heightened state of readiness. Consequently, when a cyber incident occurred, the institution was able to react swiftly, mitigating potential damage and preserving customer trust.

In contrast, ISO/IEC 27001 stands as an internationally recognized standard for information security management systems (ISMS). ISO 27001 outlines a systematic approach to managing sensitive information, encompassing the people, processes, and technology that organizations employ. The standard promotes continual improvement through a risk management process, ensuring that organizations are not just compliant but also adaptive to the ever-changing cybersecurity landscape.

For example, consider a technology firm that handles vast amounts of user data. By implementing ISO 27001, the company undertook a comprehensive review of its data handling and storage practices. They identified critical weaknesses in access controls and data encryption protocols. Following the standard’s guidance, they fortified their security measures, which not only protected customer information but also enhanced their reputation in an industry where data breaches are common. As a result, clients were more confident in entrusting their sensitive information to the firm.

On the other side of the cybersecurity compliance spectrum, PCI DSS primarily caters to organizations that handle credit card transactions. It establishes security requirements for protecting cardholder data, mandating that organizations implement specific security measures like encryption, access controls, and regular security testing. This standard is especially relevant for retail businesses and online merchants, where customer trust is paramount.

One exemplary case is an online retail operator that was initially hesitant to adopt PCI DSS due to perceived costs and complexity. Upon a data breach that exposed sensitive customer payment information, they learned the hard way that the consequences of non-compliance far outweighed the resources needed to adhere to the standard. After the breach, the organization invested in a comprehensive compliance program aligned with PCI DSS, significantly enhancing its data protection practices. Following this shift, they witnessed a marked increase in customer trust and loyalty, contributing to improved sales performance.

While NIST, ISO 27001, and PCI DSS represent prominent industry standards, several others complement these guidelines, further broadening the framework for organizational cybersecurity practices. The Health Insurance Portability and Accountability Act (HIPAA), for instance, imposes specific regulatory requirements on healthcare organizations to protect patient information. Conversely, the Federal Risk and Authorization Management Program

(FedRAMP) assures security for cloud services used by U.S. federal agencies, promoting a standardized approach to security assessments.

As industries continue to evolve, organizations must prioritize compliance with relevant standards and regulations. By adopting these frameworks, they establish a solid foundation for effective cybersecurity management. The benefits extend beyond compliance; they foster customer trust and protect brand reputation, ultimately contributing to a competitive advantage.

Implementing industry standards, however, is not without its challenges. Organizations often face hurdles related to resource allocation, staff training, and integration into existing processes. Nevertheless, overcoming these challenges is essential for organizations committed to achieving compliance and maintaining a robust cybersecurity posture.

One way organizations can address these challenges is through cross-department collaboration. For instance, involving IT, compliance, and legal teams in the implementation process fosters a holistic approach to security. This collaboration ensures that cybersecurity measures align with organizational objectives while remaining compliant with relevant industry standards. Moreover, creating interdisciplinary working groups focused on compliance can help organizations identify gaps in knowledge or processes, enabling the development of comprehensive training programs tailored to their specific needs.

Furthermore, organizations can leverage automated compliance solutions to streamline their adherence efforts.

These tools simplify tracking compliance requirements, maintain documentation, and facilitate regular audits. The adoption of technology can alleviate some burdens of compliance management, enabling staff to focus on strategic security initiatives.

Additionally, it's important for companies not to view compliance solely as a checklist. Instead, they should embrace a culture of continuous improvement and resilience in their cybersecurity posture. Engaging employees at all levels in discussions about cybersecurity best practices fosters a sense of shared responsibility and accountability. Initiatives like regular training, phishing simulations, and cybersecurity awareness campaigns can empower employees and reduce the likelihood of human error contributing to security breaches.

As organizations continue to navigate the complexities of compliance, they can take inspiration from industry peers that have successfully thrived by adhering to standards. Sharing success stories and lessons learned can serve as motivators for companies embarking on their compliance journeys. By providing tangible examples of the transformation that standards can facilitate, organizations can inspire stakeholders across various sectors to invest in compliance initiatives.

To further illustrate the impact of cyber standards, let's examine an organization from the automotive industry—a sector facing increasing scrutiny surrounding data protection, particularly as vehicles become more connected. A leading automobile manufacturer recognized the necessity of complying with the ISO 26262 standard, a crucial guideline for ensuring functional safety in automotive systems, which also incorporates cybersecurity considerations. This particular manufacturer established a dedicated team to assess cybersecurity vulnerabilities within its vehicle software architecture. By adhering to the principles set forth in this standard, the company not only mitigated risks associated with cyber threats but also enhanced customer confidence in its products' safety features.

Simultaneously, another automotive rival faced significant backlash when customer data was compromised due to a failure to integrate cybersecurity protocols while developing new vehicles. Consequently, the organization incurred substantial regulatory penalties, as well as lost customer trust and market share. The disparities in outcomes underscore the importance of adopting standards not just for regulatory compliance but also as a means of safeguarding against reputational damage.

The benefits of industry standards extend far beyond individual organizations; they establish a collective framework that enhances overall cybersecurity resilience within entire sectors. As companies adhere to these standards, they contribute to elevating security measures across the board, making their entire industry more robust against cyber threats.

One pressing concern in today's landscape is the convergence of multiple standards, which can complicate compliance processes for organizations that span various sectors. With GDPR making significant waves in data protection regulations and the emergence of new privacy laws worldwide, organizations may find themselves grappling with multiple compliance frameworks simultaneously.

To navigate this complex terrain, organizations must prioritize interoperability. Engaging in industry-specific collaborations or consortiums can provide valuable insights into harmonizing compliance processes across various standards. By sharing knowledge and experiences, organizations can work collectively to bridge the gaps between differing requirements and streamline their compliance efforts.

In conclusion, the journey to deciphering industry standards is not a mere checklist for compliance; it is a fundamental component of any organization's cybersecurity strategy. By evaluating the distinct frameworks such as NIST, ISO 27001, PCI DSS, and various others, organizations can foster resilience, enhance their security postures, and cultivate customer trust. Implementing these standards requires dedication, cross-department engagement, and a commitment to continuous improvement. With compelling case studies showcasing the practical applications and benefits of these frameworks, organizations can navigate the complexities of compliance while positioning themselves for success in an ever-evolving digital landscape.

As the cybersecurity landscape continues to change, adherence to industry standards will remain a crucial element in fostering secure organizations capable of protecting sensitive information. By committing to these frameworks, organizations not only comply with regulations but also cultivate a culture of security that ultimately supports their business objectives and enhances their credibility in the eyes of customers and stakeholders alike. In a world that increasingly prioritizes data protection, those organizations that embrace industry standards will not only survive but thrive, becoming the guardians of the digital realm.

Integrating Standards into Business Practices

In today's complex cybersecurity landscape, integrating established standards into daily business operations is not merely a regulatory obligation but an essential strategy that enhances an organization's overall security posture. Organizations often face significant challenges during this integration phase, including resistance to change, limited resources, and a lack of understanding among employees. Achieving a seamless integration of cybersecurity standards requires careful planning, effective communication, and ongoing commitment from leadership. This subchapter will provide a step-by-step guide to integrating standards such as NIST, ISO 27001, and others into organizational practices, along with insights from compliance officers who have navigated this critical process.

The first step in integrating cybersecurity standards into business practices is to understand the relevant standards that apply to the organization. Different industries may be governed by specific standards, including the Health Insurance Portability and Accountability Act (HIPAA) for healthcare organizations, the Payment Card Industry Data Security Standard (PCI DSS) for those handling payment information, and the General Data Protection Regulation (GDPR) for businesses operating within the European Union. To begin, organizations should conduct a comprehensive assessment to identify the applicable standards that pertain to their operations, stakeholders, and data types.

Following this assessment, the next step is to perform a gap analysis. This involves comparing the current cybersecurity policies and procedures to the requirements outlined in the chosen standards. A compliance officer shared their experience, stating, "When we first looked at our compliance with NIST, we realized there were several areas where our policies were insufficient. Identifying these gaps took time, but it was crucial for our success." By identifying discrepancies between current practices and the standard requirements, organizations can prioritize areas for improvement.

Next, organizations must allocate resources effectively to develop an action plan for compliance integration. This plan should detail specific tasks, responsible parties, deadlines, and required resources. Engaging cross-functional teams—including IT, legal, human resources, and operations—ensures that all aspects of the organization are covered and that everyone is on the same page regarding compliance objectives. Collaboration is key; as another compliance officer noted, "Getting input from various departments helped us understand how compliance is interwoven with our business activities."

Once a comprehensive action plan is established, organizations can begin to implement the necessary changes. This includes revising existing policies and creating new ones that align with the chosen standards. Employee training and awareness programs become increasingly important in this phase. For standards to be effectively integrated, all employees must understand the rationale behind them, their specific roles in compliance, and how to adhere to established protocols. One successful technique is to offer training sessions that incorporate real-world scenarios to demonstrate the implications of non-compliance. According to an IT manager, "Using scenarios made it relatable, and it helped everyone see that these standards weren't just 'checking boxes'—they had real consequences."

In addition to revising policies and conducting training, technology plays a vital role in supporting compliance integration. Organizations must consider how to leverage information security tools to assist in monitoring adherence to standards. This could involve adopting software that assists with risk management, threat detection, and compliance reporting. One insightful discussion revealed, "Integrating compliance tools into our existing systems made it easier to automate processes. It also reduced the overhead of documentation and tracking compliance manually."

However, it's important to highlight that while automation can streamline processes, human oversight remains crucial. Regular audits and reviews of compliance practices should be established as part of the integration process. These audits provide an opportunity to assess the effectiveness of implemented policies and controls, allowing organizations to correct any deficiencies swiftly. "We conduct regular audits, not only to satisfy compliance requirements but because it helps us learn and improve continuously," shared a compliance officer from the retail sector.

Compliance integration isn't just about policy and technology; it also hinges on fostering a culture of security awareness within the organization. Leadership must commit to making cybersecurity a core value ingrained in the organization's culture. As one executive aptly noted,

"Compliance doesn't stop with policies; it's a mindset that we need to promote across all levels of the company."

To create this culture, management should lead by example. When employees see leaders prioritizing compliance in their own actions and decision-making, they are more likely to embrace a similar mindset. A successful case study demonstrated that by regularly communicating the importance of cybersecurity and involving employees in discussions about compliance, organizations could instill a greater sense of ownership and responsibility among their staff.

Integrating standards can be fraught with challenges. Organizations frequently encounter resistance to change, often fueled by misconceptions about the complexity and burden of compliance processes. To counter this resistance, effective communication strategies must be employed. Regular updates about the integration process, the benefits it brings, and the specific expectations for employees can help alleviate concerns and foster engagement. "We found that transparent communication made a huge difference. When people understand why changes are necessary, they're much more willing to cooperate," remarked a compliance officer.

It is essential to address the concerns and questions of employees as they arise. Establishing a support structure that allows staff to voice their concerns or seek clarification can bridge the gap between management objectives and employee buy-in. This could take the form of dedicated compliance champions within each department or an anonymous feedback mechanism to ensure employees feel comfortable speaking up.

Furthermore, as organizations integrate cybersecurity standards into their practices, it's vital to remain flexible and adaptable. The cybersecurity landscape is constantly evolving, with new threats emerging and regulations changing frequently. Companies must be dedicated to continuous improvement, regularly updating policies, refining procedures, and investing in ongoing training. An executive emphasized the notion of agility: "If we rigidly adhere to a plan without considering the external environment, we risk being caught off guard. Flexibility is key to maintaining compliance."

In addition, keeping up with technological advancements and emerging cybersecurity threats can help organizations stay ahead in the compliance game. Establishing partnerships or consulting relationships with cybersecurity firms can provide valuable insights and expertise that bolster internal capabilities. Weaving in discussions during regular strategic reviews about evolving industry standards and how they affect compliance plans can also yield significant benefits.

Ultimately, the success of integrating cybersecurity standards into business practices relies on a multifaceted approach that combines strategic planning, effective communication, robust training, and cultural reinforcement. Each organization is unique, and therefore, it's critical to approach the integration process with an understanding of individual challenges and opportunities. Drawing insights from compliance officers who have successfully navigated their integration journeys can provide a roadmap for others facing similar challenges.

In conclusion, the integration of cybersecurity standards into organizational practices is a vital step toward ensuring compliance while also enhancing security resilience. By following the outlined steps of assessing standards, conducting gap analyses, developing actionable plans, and fostering a culture of security awareness, organizations can set themselves up for long-term success. As cybersecurity continues to evolve, those organizations that adapt their processes, engage their employees, and embrace a culture of continuous improvement will be best positioned to thrive in an increasingly challenging digital landscape.

The Future of Cybersecurity Standards

The landscape of cybersecurity standards is undergoing a profound transformation, driven by rapid advancements in technology and increasingly sophisticated cyber threats. As organizations strive to protect their digital assets, the regulatory environment is evolving to adapt to these changes. In this section, we will analyze emerging trends that are shaping the future of cybersecurity standards, exploring how evolving technologies and threats necessitate new compliance requirements. We will also discuss the potential impact of innovations such as artificial intelligence (AI) and blockchain on the cybersecurity landscape and provide expert predictions regarding the future of cybersecurity compliance.

One of the most significant trends in the cybersecurity standards landscape is the growing emphasis on risk management. Historically, compliance frameworks were often prescriptive, outlining specific controls and practices that organizations had to adopt. However, as technology becomes more complex and threats become more individualized, a one-size-fits-all approach to compliance is increasingly seen as inadequate. This has led to the rise of risk-based frameworks that prioritize the assessment of risks tailored to an organization's specific operations and threat landscape.

Organizations are beginning to steer away from checklists and box-ticking exercises, instead focusing on understanding their unique vulnerabilities and the potential impact of different types of cyber incidents. By adopting a risk-based approach, organizations can allocate their resources more efficiently, ensuring that their cybersecurity defenses are proportional to the threats they face. This paradigm shift is reflected in updated versions of existing standards, such as the National Institute of Standards and Technology (NIST) Cybersecurity Framework, which encourages organizations to identify, assess, and respond to risks in a customized manner.

As organizations embrace risk management, they will also need to enhance their threat intelligence capabilities. Effective risk management relies on the timely and accurate information about emerging threats, vulnerabilities, and attack vectors. This has led to a greater emphasis on the use of threat intelligence sharing platforms that allow organizations to exchange information about incidents, vulnerabilities, and indicators of compromise. The sharing of threat intelligence can facilitate a proactive rather than reactive approach to cybersecurity compliance, enabling organizations to adapt to evolving risks and to comply with regulations more effectively.

In addition to risk management, the integration of innovative technologies into organizational practices is redefining the cybersecurity compliance landscape. AI and machine learning (ML) are at the forefront, revolutionizing cybersecurity standards and practices. AI-powered tools can analyze vast amounts of data in real-time, identifying anomalous patterns and potential security breaches that would be impossible for human analysts to detect in a timely manner. Consequently, cybersecurity compliance frameworks are beginning to recognize the necessity of integrating AI-driven technologies to enhance detection, prevention, and response capabilities.

Moreover, AI can assist organizations in automatically implementing compliance protocols, reducing the potential for human error that often hinders effective cybersecurity governance. Automation tools can help organizations continuously assess compliance status, conduct audits, and remediate vulnerabilities, enabling them to meet regulatory requirements continuously rather than viewing compliance as a periodic obligation. As AI-driven solutions become more prevalent, cybersecurity standards may need to adapt by providing guidelines for the responsible use of these technologies, ensuring that organizations adopt ethical considerations alongside efficiency.

Blockchain technology also holds transformative potential for cybersecurity compliance. With its decentralized and immutable nature, blockchain can enhance the integrity and security of data, making it more difficult for cybercriminals to tamper with sensitive information. Moreover, blockchain can provide a reliable means of identity verification, allowing organizations to manage user access more securely and transparently.

As organizations look to integrate blockchain solutions into their cybersecurity practices, standards will evolve to address the specific compliance implications associated with this technology. For instance, industry standards may establish best practices for implementing blockchain-based identity verification systems, ensuring that organizations can navigate identity management challenges while remaining compliant with regulations. Similarly, cybersecurity frameworks may need to provide guidance on how organizations can effectively incorporate blockchain for data protection and auditing, harnessing its capabilities while maintaining compliance with traditional cybersecurity requirements.

The future of cybersecurity compliance will also require organizations to pay closer attention to data privacy and protection regulations. As governments across the globe implement stricter data protection laws, such as the General Data Protection Regulation (GDPR) in Europe, businesses must understand their obligations regarding the handling and processing of personal information. Compliance with these regulations necessitates not only adequate cybersecurity measures but also adjustments to organizational processes, ensuring that privacy is embedded throughout the data lifecycle.

In the coming years, cybersecurity standards will likely evolve to reflect the interconnected nature of data protection and cybersecurity. Regulations that prioritize data privacy may introduce new requirements for the encryption of personal data, incident response protocols for data breaches, and transparent reporting of data handling practices. As organizations navigate this convergence of cybersecurity and data protection, it will be essential for them to adopt a holistic compliance strategy, recognizing that compliance is not just a matter of ticking boxes but requires a comprehensive understanding of governance from multiple perspectives.

Experts predict that the need for multi-factor authentication (MFA) will continue to gain importance as cyber threats evolve. The rise of phishing attacks and credential stuffing has made traditional username and password combinations increasingly inadequate for securing sensitive information. To effectively combat these threats, standards will need to incorporate requirements for implementing MFA across critical systems and applications. As organizations adopt MFA solutions, standards can provide guidance on selecting the most appropriate methods, whether biometric authentication, security tokens, or authenticator applications, fostering best practices in identity and access management.

In addition to evolving standards for verification and access controls, the future of cybersecurity compliance will also hinge on developing effective training and awareness programs. From executives to front-line employees, everyone in an organization plays a role in maintaining cybersecurity hygiene. As organizations recognize the pivotal role of human behavior in compliance, standards will begin to emphasize the need for comprehensive training programs that focus on building a culture of security awareness. Organizations will need to prioritize engagement, creating training initiatives that resonate with employees and motivate them to adopt compliant behaviors proactively.

To address these needs, cybersecurity standards may evolve to mandate regular training and awareness initiatives, ensuring that employees at all levels are informed about the latest threats, compliance requirements, and optimal practices for safeguarding digital assets. Training programs will also need to account for the diverse range of staff, fostering tailored approaches that resonate with different roles and functions within the organization.

As we project into the future, the reality of a globalized digital environment will underscore the importance of harmonization in cybersecurity standards. Countries and regions will need to collaborate on regulatory frameworks, ensuring that compliance practices can be shared across borders seamlessly. As organizations expand their operations into new regions, centralized standards will foster cooperation, reduce compliance burdens, and help organizations align their practices with international expectations.

As standardization becomes increasingly crucial, the role of industry consortia, regulatory bodies, and cybersecurity organizations will expand. These players will collaborate to collectively establish common standards that reflect both adherence to local regulations and alignment with best practice guidelines. This unified approach will reduce the likelihood of regulatory fragmentation and enhance organizational compliance efforts.

In conclusion, the future of cybersecurity standards is intrinsically linked to several converging factors, including the rapid advancement of technology, the growing complexity of cyber threats, the emergence of new regulations, and the importance of establishing a culture of security awareness. Organizations will need to remain vigilant and adaptive, recognizing that compliance is not just a destination but an ongoing journey that requires flexibility and resilience in the face of an ever-evolving landscape. As we navigate this transformative period in cybersecurity compliance, organizations must commit to continuous improvement, leveraging innovations such as AI, blockchain, and risk management strategies to protect their digital assets effectively. By doing so, they will not only safeguard their interests but also contribute to a more secure and compliant digital world for all. The emphasis on collaboration and sharing of resources will create a robust cybersecurity ecosystem, ensuring that organizations can collectively thrive amidst rising challenges. The advances we make today will lay the groundwork for a safer cyber realm tomorrow, empowering future guardians to navigate the complexities of a dynamic and increasingly interconnected digital landscape.

Chapter 4: Mapping Your Cyber Pathway

Assessing Your Current Compliance Status

In today's digital landscape, where cyber threats are ever-present and evolving, understanding your organization's current compliance posture is critical to navigating the complexities of cybersecurity regulations. This subchapter aims to provide practical guidance on how to conduct a thorough self-assessment, equipping you with the necessary tools to identify gaps in your cybersecurity practices. With actionable templates, checklists, and real-world anecdotes, you will also see how other organizations have triumphed over compliance challenges and how they can inform your journey.

Self-assessment is the first step in moving toward a more robust compliance framework. Identifying where you currently stand lays the foundation for a comprehensive cybersecurity strategy that aligns with relevant regulations, industry standards, and best practices. Too often, organizations rush into compliance without taking the time to evaluate their existing posture, which can lead to oversights, incomplete strategies, and, ultimately, regulatory failures.

Understanding Your Current Compliance Status

The first step in evaluating your compliance status is to create a clear understanding of existing regulations, industry standards, and cybersecurity frameworks relevant to your organization. Depending on your industry, these could include regulations such as the General Data Protection Regulation (GDPR), the Health Insurance Portability and Accountability Act (HIPAA), or the Payment Card Industry Data Security Standard (PCI DSS). Familiarizing yourself with these regulations gives you a set of criteria against which you can measure your current practices.

A compliance gap analysis is a valuable tool to begin this assessment process. It allows organizations to identify differences between what is required by regulations and what is currently implemented. Here is a simple template to guide your gap analysis:

Gap Analysis Template

1. Regulatory/Standards Requirement:

Specify the regulation or standard you are assessing.

2. Current Compliance Status:

Describe your organization's current practices related to this requirement.

3. Gaps Identified:

List any gaps between the requirement and your current practices.

4. Action Required:

Outline the steps needed to close these gaps.

5. Responsible Party:

Identify who will be responsible for addressing each gap.

This template serves as a roadmap for organizations aiming to ensure they meet their legal obligations while also safeguarding sensitive data.

Armed with a gap analysis template, you can assess your organization's cybersecurity practices. Keep in mind that your assessment should cover multiple facets of cybersecurity compliance, including data privacy policies, incident response plans, access control mechanisms, employee training programs, and third-party vendor management.

For instance, let's take a look at a healthcare organization that engaged in a comprehensive self-assessment process. 'HealthCare Plus,' a fictitious organization, understood that compliance with HIPAA regulations was non-negotiable, not just for legal reasons but also for maintaining the trust of its patients.

Upon conducting their self-assessment, HealthCare Plus identified that while they had implemented electronic health record (EHR) systems, they had not fully secured all access points, thereby risking unauthorized data access. By applying the gap analysis template, they were able to pinpoint the need for multifactor authentication and implemented a new protocol that included mandatory employee training for using these systems effectively.

Identifying gaps is essential, but it becomes even more challenging when organizations lack comprehensive documentation of existing procedures. A well-documented compliance framework can be a game-changer in this phase. As you assess your organization's current practices, gather proper documentation for all existing policies, protocols, and incident reports. This documentation will not only help in identifying gaps but will also be invaluable during external audits and assessments.

Utilizing Checklists for Comprehensive Assessment

Checklists are invaluable tools in any compliance assessment process. They can guide you to ensure that no critical areas are overlooked, providing a structured approach to evaluating your compliance state. Here is a checklist that touches on critical aspects of cybersecurity compliance:

Self-Assessment Compliance Checklist

1. Data Inventory:

- Have you identified all personal and sensitive data that your organization collects, processes, and stores?

- Are there any data retention policies in place?

2. Access Control:

- Do you have a policy that defines user access levels?

- Is there a process for regularly reviewing access permissions?

3. Incident Response:

- Do you have a documented incident response plan?

- Is the incident response plan regularly tested through simulations?

4. Employee Training:

- Are there mandatory training programs on data protection and cybersecurity for all employees?

- How often are these training programs reviewed and updated?

5. Vendor Management:

- Are your third-party vendors assessed for compliance with relevant regulations?

- Do you have contracts that obligate vendors to adhere to specific security requirements?

This checklist serves as a baseline. Depending on your industry and specific regulatory requirements, additional items may be tailored to fit your unique business context. The act of checking each box not only empowers your team and gives them a sense of accomplishment but also highlights the areas that require immediate focus.

Engaging Anecdotes from Real-World Assessments

Understanding abstract concepts through real-life stories is a powerful way to illustrate challenges and the successes that come from diligent compliance efforts. Consider the story of 'TechForces Inc.,' a tech company unsure of its compliance standing regarding the General Data Protection Regulation (GDPR). Initially, TechForces had undertaken a self-assessment without a clear understanding of the GDPR's intricate requirements.

After realizing that their customer data handling processes fell short of compliance, the team organized a series of focused workshops. By bringing in GDPR experts, they were able to fill knowledge gaps within their team. The outcome? Not only did they successfully align their practices with GDPR, but they also created a sustained culture of compliance within the organization.

Success stories like this underline the importance of both self-assessment and the willingness to seek external expertise when required. Engaging stakeholders across your organization in the assessment process can reveal critical insights. Using cross-functional teams that include members from IT, HR, Legal, and Business Operations fosters collaborative thinking and empowers individuals across departments to contribute to the organization's compliance journey.

Transforming Challenges into Opportunities

While the self-assessment process can seem daunting, particularly in identifying areas for improvement, it's important to view these challenges as opportunities. Consider the story of 'RetailCom,' a retail organization that learned the hard way how essential compliance assessments were when they faced a significant data breach due to lax protocols.

Following the breach, RetailCom recognized that their initial self-assessment should have been more thorough and consultative. They revamped their entire compliance process, integrating lessons learned from the breach into their assessment process. This proactive approach not only allowed them to tighten their cybersecurity practices but also elevated their reputation in the eyes of customers and regulators alike.

Empowerment through Understanding

As you embark on your self-assessment journey, remember that understanding your starting point is crucial. Recognizing gaps, collecting documentation, and utilizing checklists and templates not only arms you with actionable insights but also empowers you to take ownership of your organization's compliance strategy. This empowerment can lead to a stronger military of cybersecurity champions ready to protect the organization from day-to-day operational risks and future regulatory challenges.

Finally, it's essential to communicate the results of your self-assessment transparently within your organization. Share insights with your executive team, employees, and relevant stakeholders to reinforce the importance of compliance as a collective responsibility. This transparency not only builds a culture of accountability but also spreads awareness about the measures necessary to create a secure environment.

Moving Forward

With your self-assessment completed and a clearer understanding of your compliance landscape, you will be better equipped to craft a tailored compliance strategy. Knowing your organization's gaps and strengths provides a strategic foundation essential for your cybersecurity pathway. Moreover, continue to revisit this self-assessment process regularly to maintain agility and responsiveness in the face of regulatory changes and evolving cyber threats.

Through thoughtful self-assessment, empowerment, and shared understanding, you lay the groundwork for a robust cybersecurity framework that not only meets compliance obligations but fosters trust and assurance among stakeholders and customers alike.

Crafting a Tailored Compliance Strategy

In today's rapidly evolving digital landscape, crafting a tailored compliance strategy is paramount for organizations seeking to protect their sensitive data, maintain customer trust, and uphold regulatory obligations. A well-structured compliance strategy not only provides a framework for organizational success but also harmonizes with business goals, operational practices, and risk appetite. This subchapter will guide readers through the essential components of developing a personalized compliance strategy, incorporating insights and examples from successful organizations and cybersecurity experts.

Understanding the foundations of compliance is the first step in creating a strategy that resonates with your organization's mission. Compliance is not merely a box-ticking exercise; it is an ongoing commitment to uphold the principles of accountability, transparency, and ethical conduct. Hence, developing a compliance strategy goes beyond meeting regulations; it involves fundamentally aligning with your organization's vision to foster a culture of cybersecurity awareness and proactive risk management.

Assessing Organizational Goals and Risk Tolerance

Before embarking on the compliance journey, it is vital to identify and articulate your organization's goals and risk tolerance. These elements will serve as the cornerstone for your tailored compliance strategy.

Organizational goals should encompass the broader vision of what the organization aspires to achieve. This may encompass objectives such as expanding into new markets, enhancing customer experience, or improving operational efficiency. For example, a financial institution might prioritize customer data protection as a way to build trust and loyalty among clients, making compliance with regulations like the Gramm-Leach-Bliley Act (GLBA) a key focus of their compliance strategy.

Risk tolerance, on the other hand, refers to the level of risk that an organization is willing to accept in pursuit of its goals. This includes a comprehensive assessment of potential cyber threats, vulnerabilities, and the implications of non-compliance. An organization dedicated to innovation, for instance, may accept a higher level of risk associated with new technology adoption while implementing tailored controls to mitigate these risks effectively.

To assess both organizational goals and risk tolerance, organizations can employ tools such as SWOT (Strengths, Weaknesses, Opportunities, and Threats) analyses, stakeholder interviews, and risk assessments. Once these foundational elements are clear, you can move toward developing your compliance strategy.

Step-by-Step Guidance to Developing the Strategy

1. Establish a Cross-Functional Team: The foundation of an effective compliance strategy lies in collaboration. Form a cross-functional team that encompasses various

departments such as IT, legal, compliance, operations, and human resources. This team will be tasked with identifying compliance needs, assessing risks, and framing the strategy to ensure that all perspectives are considered. Including stakeholders from different departments fosters a sense of ownership and helps integrate compliance into the organizational culture.

2. Conduct a Compliance Gap Analysis: Following the formation of your team, it's essential to perform a compliance gap analysis. This entails comparing the current state of your organization's compliance posture to the required regulatory standards and benchmarks. Identify gaps in policies, procedures, and practices that need to be addressed to meet these standards.

For example, consider a healthcare organization evaluating its compliance with the Health Insurance Portability and Accountability Act (HIPAA). Through a gap analysis, the team may discover that while the organization has stringent data access controls, its employee training on privacy policies is insufficient. Closing this gap will be crucial to maintaining compliance.

3. Define Clear Policies and Procedures: Based on the findings from the gap analysis, develop and document clear policies and procedures that align with regulatory requirements and organizational goals. Policies should provide a framework for compliance, detailing roles and responsibilities, incident response protocols, and data protection measures. Procedures should outline the specific steps required to execute these policies effectively.

4. Create a Training and Awareness Program: Once policies and procedures are established, implement a training and awareness program aimed at educating employees about compliance obligations and best practices. This program should be tailored to address the unique needs and roles of various stakeholders within the organization.

Engage employees through interactive training sessions, e-learning modules, and compliance nuggets in team meetings. Incorporate real-world scenarios and case studies to illustrate the importance of compliance and the potential consequences of lapses. For instance, a retail organization may share stories of data breaches that occurred due to employee negligence, fostering a culture of accountability and vigilance.

5. Implement Monitoring and Reporting Mechanisms: Monitoring is a crucial component of a compliance strategy, allowing organizations to track adherence to policies and identify areas needing improvement. Establish metrics to measure compliance effectiveness and develop reporting mechanisms to disseminate results to stakeholders. Regular audits, testing of controls, and incident reviews should be part of the monitoring process.

For example, consider a technology company that implements periodic audits of its software development practices to ensure they align with data protection regulations. These audits can uncover any deviations from policies and help the organization continuously improve its compliance posture.

6. Adapt and Evolve the Strategy: The digital landscape is in constant flux, and so are compliance requirements.

Therefore, it is essential to view your compliance strategy as a living document that must adapt to changing regulations, emerging technologies, and evolving business objectives. Regularly review and update your compliance strategy to ensure its continued relevance.

This may include integrating new compliance frameworks or shifting focus in response to new threats and vulnerabilities. For instance, the emergence of Internet of Things (IoT) devices may necessitate updates to a compliance strategy focused on data security, triggering a re-evaluation of policies governing connected devices.

Engaging Stakeholders for Buy-In and Commitment

A successful compliance strategy requires the engagement and commitment of all stakeholders in the organization. This means promoting open communication about compliance goals, strategies, and benefits at every organizational level.

Leadership buy-in is particularly crucial. Executives and management must champion compliance initiatives by reinforcing their significance to the organization's overall success. By linking compliance with corporate objectives such as customer trust, competitive advantage, and risk management, leaders can cultivate a culture that prioritizes compliance.

Moreover, they should consider establishing a compliance committee that connects stakeholders from various departments, enhancing communication and collaboration. This committee can serve as a forum for discussing challenges, sharing progress updates, and identifying opportunities for compliance innovations.

Balancing Compliance and Business Innovation

In crafting a compliance strategy, organizations must navigate the fine line between regulatory adherence and business innovation. While compliance is essential, it is crucial not to stifle innovation or responsiveness that fuels growth. Organizations should recognize that compliance can coexist with progressive business strategies when approached thoughtfully and strategically.

For example, a financial services firm launching a new digital product can strategically align its compliance framework to accommodate innovation by implementing agile compliance practices. This allows the organization to remain compliant while adapting to rapid changes in the industry.

One strategy to achieve this balance is through risk-based assessments during the innovation process. When developing new products or services, organizations can conduct compliance assessments early, identifying potential regulatory hurdles and proactively addressing them. This approach fosters agility while maintaining adherence, enabling organizations to innovate without compromising their compliance commitments.

Moreover, engaging in dialogue with regulators and industry associations can pave the way for understanding evolving standards and compliance expectations. This proactive approach helps organizations navigate regulatory environments while fostering innovation, ultimately contributing to a more resilient financial and operational framework.

Successful Examples of Tailored Compliance Strategies

1. Example 1: The Financial Institution: A mid-sized bank recognized the need to strengthen its cybersecurity posture to align with new regulatory standards following an increase in cyber threats. By forming a cross-functional team, the bank conducted a thorough compliance gap analysis and identified areas for improvement in its customer data protection practices.

The bank designed a tailored compliance strategy that included robust encryption protocols, comprehensive employee training, and regular audits. The program not only addressed regulatory requirements but also enhanced customer trust and confidence. As a result, the institution not only achieved compliance but also increased its customer base by demonstrating a strong commitment to safeguarding sensitive financial data.

2. Example 2: The Healthcare Provider: A healthcare organization faced challenges in meeting HIPAA compliance requirements due to varying levels of employee awareness and inconsistent practices across departments. By establishing a compliance task force that included representatives from IT, legal, and operations, the organization created a training and awareness program tailored to different employee roles.

The task force developed clear policies that outlined patient data handling procedures and integrated regular training sessions. By fostering a culture of accountability around compliance, the organization significantly reduced the risk of breaches and enhanced its overall operational efficiency.

3. Example 3: The Tech Startup: A technology startup specializing in IoT devices aimed to disrupt the market through innovative product offerings. However, the founders recognized the importance of compliance with emerging data protection regulations. They established a compliance framework early in their development process by conducting regular risk assessments of their products and protocols.

Engaging in direct conversations with industry regulators, the startup implemented best practices that allowed for flexibility and adaptation within its product development process. This proactive approach enabled the startup to launch its products quickly while ensuring compliance, illustrating a successful balance between innovation and adherence.

Conclusion

Crafting a tailored compliance strategy is essential for organizations striving to safeguard their digital assets and foster trust with stakeholders. By aligning compliance with organizational goals, employing a step-by-step approach, engaging a cross-functional team, and striking a balance between compliance and innovation, organizations can position themselves for sustained success in the digital realm.

Cybersecurity compliance is not an ever-static obligation but rather an ongoing journey, necessitating regular reassessment and adaptation to remain effective in an ever-evolving landscape. Through commitment at all levels and a comprehensive strategy, organizations can thrive while ensuring compliance becomes an integral part of their fabric rather than just an additional burden. As they navigate this complex terrain, organizations will not only protect their interests but also emerge as leaders committed to ethical, responsible behavior in the digital age.

Implementing and Monitoring Your Strategy

In the dynamic realm of cybersecurity compliance, crafting an effective implementation strategy is crucial for organizations wishing to safeguard sensitive data while aligning with regulatory requirements. The implementation phase is where abstract compliance goals transform into tangible actions. This subchapter delves into the practical aspects of executing a comprehensive compliance strategy, emphasizing resource allocation, timeline creation, and performance monitoring.

As organizations initiate their journey toward compliance, understanding the significance of continuous assessment and adaptation is fundamental. The threat landscape is constantly evolving, and so too must compliance measures. By examining real-life case studies of organizations that faced various implementation challenges, readers will glean valuable insights and strategies for overcoming common obstacles.

Resource Allocation

Effective resource allocation is the cornerstone of any successful compliance strategy. Without adequate resources—be it personnel, budget, or technology—organizations may struggle to implement necessary controls or foster a culture of compliance. The first step in the resource allocation process involves conducting a thorough assessment of existing assets and resources.

Organizations should begin by identifying key personnel responsible for compliance roles. This includes IT staff, compliance officers, and legal advisors who will play critical roles in shaping and enforcing the compliance strategy. By establishing a compliance team, organizations can ensure a collaborative approach to navigating the complexities of cybersecurity regulations and standards.

Beyond human resources, organizations must allocate financial resources to support compliance initiatives. This may require a detailed budget that accounts for training programs, technological solutions, and external consulting services if necessary. It is essential to highlight the return on investment (ROI) for compliance-related expenditures by illustrating how they mitigate the risks of data breaches and regulatory fines.

The allocation of technological resources should not be overlooked. Organizations have a plethora of tools and software at their disposal to enhance their compliance efforts. From automated compliance monitoring tools to advanced threat detection systems, investing in the right technology can significantly streamline operations and bolster security efforts.

Timeline Creation

Once resources have been allocated, the next step is to create a realistic timeline that outlines the various phases of the compliance strategy implementation. This timeline should encompass key milestones, deadlines, and deliverables, allowing organizations to track their progress effectively.

When developing a compliance timeline, organizations should consider the following steps:

1. Defining Objectives: Clearly articulate the specific compliance objectives to be achieved within a defined timeframe. For example, these objectives may include achieving compliance with GDPR within six months or completing a risk assessment within three months.

2. Creating a Work Breakdown Structure: Break down the implementation process into smaller, manageable tasks. Assign responsibilities to relevant team members and establish dependencies between tasks to ensure a logical workflow.

3. Establishing Milestones: Identify key milestones within the implementation timeline. Milestones act as checkpoints to evaluate progress and make necessary adjustments. Examples of milestones may include the completion of a risk assessment, finalization of data protection policies, or successful audits.

4. Including Buffer Time: Given the unpredictable nature of compliance tasks, organizations should include buffer time within their timeline. Allowing for unforeseen challenges can

prevent unnecessary stress and ensure that the implementation remains on track.

5. Communication Plans: Establish regular communication across the compliance team and stakeholders. Frequent updates on the status of implementation can increase transparency and facilitate collaboration.

Once the timeline is established, consistency in adherence to deadlines is critical. Stakeholders must remain vigilant and hold team members accountable for meeting their responsibilities.

Performance Monitoring

Regular performance monitoring is vital for maintaining compliance within a rapidly changing landscape. Performance indicators should be incorporated into the implementation strategy, allowing organizations to gauge their effectiveness. By monitoring progress, organizations can make informed decisions on where to adjust strategies and allocate resources for maximum impact.

Key performance indicators (KPIs) for compliance strategies may include:

1. Completion Rates: Track the completion rates of compliance assessments, training programs, and policy updates. High completion rates may indicate successful engagement and adherence to compliance training.

2. Incidence of Non-Compliance: Monitor the number of instances of non-compliance identified through audits or assessments. A decrease in non-compliance incidents may suggest that implementation strategies are effective.

3. Incident Response Times: Measure the time taken to respond to security incidents or breaches. Reduced response times signify improvements in incident management capabilities, which is a crucial aspect of compliance.

4. Employee Awareness Levels: Conduct regular surveys to assess employees' understanding of compliance policies and their confidence in compliance practices. Higher awareness levels translate to a more robust culture of compliance.

5. Audit Findings: Review audit results and any findings from third-party assessments. These findings will help organizations identify weaknesses in their compliance posture.

By regularly tracking these performance indicators, organizations will gain insights into what areas require improvement and how resources can be better allocated. Performance monitoring is not a one-time effort, but an ongoing process that demands attention.

Case Studies of Successful Implementation

To solidify the practical aspects of implementing a compliance strategy, it's essential to examine real-life case studies of organizations that have navigated this complex landscape.

One notable example is that of a mid-sized financial services company that faced challenges in compliance with the General Data Protection Regulation (GDPR). Initially, the company lacked a cohesive strategy and struggled with resource allocation, often leading to confusion among employees regarding compliance roles and expectations.

Recognizing the need for a formal compliance strategy, the organization appointed a dedicated Compliance Officer to lead efforts. This officer conducted an assessment of existing resources, clarifying team roles and responsibilities. Importantly, the financial department allocated a budget specifically for compliance initiatives, which included employee training, consultancy services, and GDPR compliance software.

Creating a comprehensive implementation timeline with clearly defined objectives led to the identification of critical milestones. The company implemented monthly progress reviews and communicated updates regularly to team members. This proactive approach allowed them to stay on track and address potential challenges before they became significant setbacks.

As a result of their effort, the financial services company achieved GDPR compliance within the six-month timeline while cultivating a culture of compliance among employees. Regular performance monitoring revealed a significant reduction in compliance-related incidents and an increase in employee understanding of data protection practices.

In contrast, examining a manufacturing firm that failed to adopt similar proactive measures provides valuable lessons as well. This organization faced major non-compliance issues with the Health Insurance Portability and Accountability Act (HIPAA). Over the years, the absence of a structured compliance strategy led to a series of security breaches, resulting in financial penalties and reputational damage.

By neglecting to allocate necessary resources for HIPAA compliance, the manufacturing firm faced significant repercussions. Their failure to create a comprehensive timeline exacerbated the situation, leading to missed deadlines and compliance objectives. This case serves as a stark reminder of the importance of structured resource allocation and timeline adherence in the compliance journey.

Strategies for Continuous Improvement

While successful implementation serves as a foundation for compliance, the quest for continuous improvement is vital for adapting to the ever-changing threat landscape. Organizations should not consider compliance as a one-time achievement; instead, they should adopt a culture of ongoing evaluation and refinement.

The following strategies can help foster continuous improvement in compliance practices:

1. Regular Training and Awareness Programs: Providing ongoing training to employees ensures that they remain informed about compliance requirements and best practices. Organizations should integrate awareness programs into their continuous learning culture, promoting knowledge sharing and skill enhancement.

2. Feedback Mechanisms: Establish feedback mechanisms that encourage employees to share their thoughts on compliance policies and procedures. Gathering input from individuals at all levels enhances the compliance framework's effectiveness, as employees possess firsthand insights into the organizational culture.

3. Scheduled Review Cycles: Organizations should implement periodic reviews of compliance strategies, performance indicators, and policies. These reviews present opportunities to assess whether compliance measures are meeting expectations and whether adjustments are required.

4. Stakeholder Involvement: Involve stakeholders in the assessment and review processes, as engagement fosters ownership of compliance efforts. By including diverse perspectives, organizations can refine their strategies to better align with the needs and concerns of various departments.

5. Adopting External Benchmarks: Engaging external benchmarks, such as industry standards, can provide organizations with essential guidance on best practices. Learning from industry peers or adopting exemplary standards places organizations in a stronger position to enhance their compliance strategies.

6. Leveraging Technological Solutions: As technology continues to evolve, organizations should remain open to integrating advanced solutions that strengthen compliance efforts. Implementing technologies that automate monitoring, risk assessments, and reporting can reduce human error and expedite responses.

7. Celebrating Achievements: Acknowledging and celebrating compliance milestones encourages a culture of vigilance. Organizations should create incentives for effective compliance practices—an approach that fosters motivation and collective responsibility toward achieving compliance goals.

In summary, implementing and monitoring a cybersecurity compliance strategy involves a multifaceted approach that requires thoughtful resource allocation, clear timelines, and continuous assessment. By examining real-world case studies and emphasizing the importance of fostering continuous improvement, organizations can enhance their compliance efforts and remain agile in a fluctuating digital landscape. In an environment where cyber threats are increasingly sophisticated, grounded and adaptable compliance practices are fundamental in safeguarding sensitive data and protecting organizational integrity.

Chapter 5: Case Studies: Learning from the Guardians

Success Stories in Compliance

In the digital landscape, achieving compliance with cybersecurity regulations and standards is not merely a checkbox exercise but a crucial endeavor that can significantly enhance an organization's resilience and credibility. Through the lens of organizational commitment, strategic planning, and innovative approaches, this section sheds light on several exemplary organizations that have successfully navigated the intricate world of compliance. Each case study not only reveals the methodologies employed but also highlights the challenges faced, providing a roadmap for others aspiring to secure their digital assets.

One illustrative example comes from a global healthcare organization, HealthSecure Inc., which faced stringent compliance requirements under HIPAA (Health Insurance Portability and Accountability Act). The company, which manages patient records for over a million individuals, recognized the severe consequences of non-compliance, including hefty fines and loss of customer trust.

To tackle these challenges, HealthSecure initiated a comprehensive risk assessment process. "We started with a thorough evaluation of our existing security infrastructure," said Jennifer Lee, the company's Chief Compliance Officer.

"This helped us identify vulnerabilities and areas that needed immediate attention." HealthSecure adopted the NIST (National Institute of Standards and Technology) Cybersecurity Framework as a guiding instrument to develop its compliance strategy.

The organization engaged all stakeholders, from IT and legal teams to front-line staff, ensuring that everyone understood their role in maintaining compliance. Through tailored training sessions, HealthSecure reinforced the importance of safeguarding patient information. "It was crucial for us to cultivate a culture of accountability and awareness at every level," Lee explained.

After implementing these measures, HealthSecure not only achieved compliance but saw a significant increase in patient trust as evidenced by a 30% rise in customer satisfaction scores within a year. "Compliance isn't just a requirement; it has become a cornerstone of our relationship with our patients," she added.

In a different industry sector, a financial services company, SecureFinance Corp., faced its own set of compliance hurdles with both PCI DSS (Payment Card Industry Data Security Standard) and GDPR (General Data Protection Regulation) looming over its operations. The organization realized that merely meeting the minimum requirements would not be sufficient; rather, it needed to transform its approach to embed security and compliance into its business processes.

John Carter, the Chief Information Security Officer at SecureFinance, emphasized the importance of a proactive approach. “We weren’t satisfied with just checking off boxes.

We wanted to set a benchmark for compliance that would elevate our entire security posture." SecureFinance invested in new technologies, including advanced encryption protocols and AI-driven analytics, to enhance its security measures.

To ensure compliance with GDPR, SecureFinance conducted comprehensive data mapping to understand where customer data resided and how it was being processed. "Data privacy is paramount to building trust with our customers," stated Carter. "By implementing clearly defined data handling policies, we not only complied with GDPR but positioned ourselves as leaders in data protection within the financial sector."

The organizational changes following this commitment resulted in a notable 40% reduction in security incidents and a strengthened reputation in an industry increasingly scrutinized for data-dependent operations. Carter elucidated, "The dividends of our investment in compliance have been multifaceted; we've seen a boost in customer confidence, stronger partnerships, and a clear differentiation from our competitors."

In the realm of e-commerce, QuickBuy, an online retail giant, faced the challenge of navigating a myriad of compliance issues, particularly surrounding data breaches and customer data protection. A significant incident in the industry served as a wake-up call for the organization, prompting a deep dive into their existing practices.

"After witnessing a competitor suffer a major data breach, we had to act swiftly," recalled Laura Thompson, QuickBuy's Compliance Director. "We formed a cross-functional task force to audit our systems and protocols. It was a no-nonsense approach because our brand was at stake."

QuickBuy implemented a multifaceted strategy that included upgrading its technology infrastructure, adopting stricter access controls, and enhancing incident response protocols. Through this transformation, Thompson stated, "We not only met compliance requirements, but we also improved our overall security posture. Our team was trained to be vigilant, and cybersecurity became a shared responsibility rather than just an IT issue."

The financial outcomes were promising: QuickBuy reported a 25% increase in sales post-implementation, alongside a dramatic decrease in customer complaints related to data security. "Compliance has empowered us to be more customer-centric; our shoppers feel secure, and that translates to loyalty," Thompson noted.

Shifting focus to the energy sector, GreenFuture Power faced unique challenges related to compliance with environmental regulations and cybersecurity measures to protect critical infrastructure. The company's complexities were heightened by the increasing sophistication of cyber threats targeting essential services.

To address these, GreenFuture took a holistic approach, merging compliance with its corporate sustainability initiatives. “Our mission is to serve the community and protect the environment, and that extends to how we handle data and security," said Elena Martinez, GreenFuture’s Chief Risk Officer. The organization undertook an extensive risk assessment that integrated environmental compliance with cybersecurity initiatives, resulting in a comprehensive action plan.

Martinez highlighted the importance of collaboration with regulators and industry peers to share best practices. “We formed a consortium with other energy companies to develop a unified approach to compliance and cybersecurity," she explained. This partnership not only facilitated knowledge sharing but also enabled the company to stay abreast of emerging regulatory changes.

The proactive measures led to successful compliance with both federal energy regulations and cybersecurity standards. GreenFuture noted a decrease in both operational risks and compliance costs by over 20%. “Our investment in compliance has not just been about avoiding penalties; it’s about fostering resilience and innovation in our organization,” concluded Martinez.

Looking across international borders, TechGlobal, a multinational technology firm, encountered substantial difficulties aligning its operations with diverse compliance requirements in multiple jurisdictions, particularly related to data protection laws like GDPR and CCPA (California Consumer Privacy Act). The complexity of managing various data regulations led to significant operational burdens.

“Compliance shouldn’t feel like a hindrance; it should be an opportunity to streamline processes,” suggested David Harper, TechGlobal's Compliance Lead. To tackle the multitude of requirements, TechGlobal established a centralized compliance framework that allowed it to standardize practices globally while retaining flexibility for local laws.

Through automating compliance procedures, TechGlobal achieved significant efficiencies. Harper described the realization: "Once we integrated compliance as a core component of our business strategy, we found that it enhanced rather than obstructed our innovation efforts."

The results were tangible. TechGlobal reported a 50% reduction in compliance-related costs and improved speed-to-market for new products and services. "Investing in compliance has become a strategic advantage for us; it allows us to focus on innovation while ensuring we are meeting our legal obligations," Harper affirmed.

In the world of education, LearnNow, a leading online education provider, faced regulatory scrutiny regarding student data privacy and security. The pressure resulted from both federal regulations and individual state laws, requiring a rigorous approach to compliance.

Recognizing the implications of non-compliance for its operations, the leadership team initiated a complete overhaul of its data protection policies. "Education is about trust, and we realized that protecting our students' information was paramount," stated Sarah Kim, LearnNow's Chief Information Officer. Collaborating closely with legal advisors, LearnNow developed a suite of training modules for its educators to empower them with knowledge about data privacy.

Through rigorous audits and the implementation of multi-factor authentication across all platforms, LearnNow succeeded in not only meeting compliance requirements but enhancing its overall security. Kim observed, "What started as a compliance challenge turned into a platform for us to build stronger relationships with our students."

The financial impact was significant; LearnNow reported a 30% increase in enrollment after these initiatives were undertaken, highlighting the necessity of compliance for organizational credibility. “Compliance has demonstrated to our students and their families that we take their security seriously, reinforcing their decision to join our learning community,” Kim concluded.

These success stories illustrate a common theme: a steadfast commitment to cybersecurity compliance not only resolves regulatory challenges but also creates a foundation for growth, innovation, and trust. The steps taken by these exemplary organizations reinforce the notion that compliance is not a hindrance but rather a pathway toward greater security and operational excellence. Through resilience, adaptability, and strategic foresight, these organizations serve as guiding lights in the continuously evolving landscape of cybersecurity.

In each case, the leaders understood that compliance could no longer be viewed as an isolated objective but must be integrated into every facet of organizational strategy, transforming it into a competitive advantage. As organizations continue to navigate the labyrinth of compliance, these success stories serve as both inspiration and a practical framework to follow. The dedication exhibited by these guardians of the digital realm underscores the importance of fostering a culture where compliance is not simply about adherence, but about advancing the safeguarding of digital assets for the betterment of their customers and the communities they serve.

Failures and Lessons Learned

The realm of cybersecurity is littered with cautionary tales, showcasing the dire repercussions of non-compliance. Organizations, both large and small, have stumbled into the abyss of catastrophic failures, primarily due to preventable mistakes and lapses in vigilance. These stories serve as potent reminders of the vital importance of adhering to cybersecurity regulations and best practices. In this section, we will dissect several notable failures, highlight the specific missteps that led to their downfall, and offer invaluable lessons learned for organizations navigating the complex cybersecurity landscape.

One of the most infamous examples of non-compliance consequences is the case of Equifax, one of the largest credit reporting agencies in the world. In 2017, Equifax experienced a massive data breach that exposed the personal information of approximately 147 million individuals. The breach was a result of failure to patch a known vulnerability in Apache Struts, an open-source web application framework. This vulnerability had been publicly disclosed months before the attack, giving Equifax ample time to address the issue. However, the company failed to implement the necessary security updates, which ultimately allowed attackers to infiltrate their systems and gain access to sensitive customer data, including Social Security numbers and credit card information.

In the aftermath of the breach, Equifax faced severe repercussions. The company experienced significant reputational damage as consumers expressed outrage over the mishandling of their sensitive information. Trust, once lost, is difficult to regain. As part of the fallout, Equifax was required to pay at least $700 million in fines and settlement costs to affected individuals, regulatory bodies, and consumers, marking one of the largest payouts for a data breach in history. More than just a financial loss, the breach illuminated the importance of a proactive approach to cybersecurity compliance. Organizations must remain vigilant, continuously updating their security protocols to address emerging threats and vulnerabilities.

The case of Target, a retail giant, serves as another sobering reminder of the potential consequences of neglecting compliance. In late 2013, Target experienced a breach that compromised the credit and debit card information of approximately 40 million customers, along with personal information of an additional 70 million individuals. Investigations revealed that hackers gained access to Target's network through a third-party vendor, an HVAC vendor that had valid access credentials. The incident happened as a result of Target's failure to adhere to the Payment Card Industry Data Security Standards (PCI DSS).

Upon deeper analysis, it became evident that Target had several security shortcomings. The company had implemented an intrusion detection system, but it failed to respond adequately to the alerts generated by this system. Moreover, encryption methods used by Target to protect cardholder data were not robust enough, leaving the information vulnerable to attackers. The aftermath included significant financial repercussions, estimated to exceed $200 million, as well as lasting damage to the brand's reputation. Target learned the hard way that neglecting cybersecurity compliance not only exposes organizations to severe financial penalties but can also result in a long and challenging recovery process in regaining customer trust.

The fallout from these incidents underscores the importance of a comprehensive cybersecurity strategy that encompasses not just technology but also people and processes. Organizations cannot afford to view compliance as a one-time effort but must embrace a culture of continuous improvement and vigilance. This theme is evident in the case of Yahoo!, which suffered a series of massive data breaches over several years, ultimately leading to a significant loss in value and trust. The breaches, which affected all three billion of Yahoo!'s user accounts, were attributed to outdated security protocols, failure to encrypt sensitive data, and a lack of timely disclosures regarding breaches.

Yahoo!'s failings demonstrate the need for clarity and openness in cybersecurity practices. The company's decision to wait several years before revealing the full extent of the breaches not only inflamed public outrage but also drew scrutiny from regulators. In 2017, the company was forced to pay $35 million to settle a class-action lawsuit and ultimately faced a severe decrease in acquisition valuation when Verizon acquired Yahoo! for a reduced price of $4.48 billion. This case emphasizes the critical need for transparency in cybersecurity practices, regulatory compliance, and data protection measures. Organizations must implement robust response plans, ensuring swift notification of breaches to stakeholders, thereby demonstrating a commitment to protecting user data and fostering trust.

As we analyze these catastrophic failures, a distinct pattern emerges: organizations experience non-compliance repercussions when they neglect the fundamentals of cybersecurity hygiene. In the case of Capital One, a financial services company, a cloud misconfiguration led to the exposure of over 100 million customer accounts, due to weaknesses in security controls on their Amazon Web Services (AWS) infrastructure. The breach was attributed to a failure to adhere to best practices for accessing and managing data in the cloud. A former employee exploited this misconfiguration to extract sensitive personal information, resulting in significant financial consequences and regulatory scrutiny.

Capital One's case highlights the importance of formalized cybersecurity training for employees, as well as robust third-party risk assessments. Developing strong security controls around cloud services and ensuring that developers and IT staff are adequately trained to recognize the risks associated with cloud misconfigurations are crucial steps that organizations must undertake to mitigate the chance of recurring mishaps. The financial fallout was severe, as Capital One faced over $80 million in fines from the Office of the Comptroller of the Currency (OCC) and a class-action lawsuit from affected users.

Moreover, as organizations broaden their operational scope with cloud-based solutions, the complexity of compliance grows. Businesses must remain informed and adaptable, continuously updating their practices to incorporate evolving regulations such as GDPR, which mandates stringent oversight of user data and privacy. In 2018, British Airways was dealt a record £183 million fine by the Information Commissioner's Office (ICO) for a data breach that exposed the personal and credit card details of over 500,000 customers. The breach stemmed from a failure to secure a vulnerability in their payment page.

British Airways' shortcomings not only involved a failure to implement essential security measures but also brought to light the issues of rapid digital transformation and insufficient leadership oversight regarding cybersecurity compliance. The incident serves as a reminder that even established organizations can falter when they do not prioritize compliance as an integral component of their business operations. The repercussions of such failures transcend immediate financial penalties; they significantly impact the organization's operational integrity and public perception.

Equally important are the lessons learned from healthcare organizations that have faced serious consequences due to non-compliance with HIPAA regulations. In 2015, Anthem, one of the largest health insurance providers in the United States, experienced a massive data breach resulting in the exposure of 78.8 million individuals' health records. The breach resulted from weak security protocols and vulnerabilities tied to social engineering attacks targeting employees. In the aftermath, Anthem faced over $16 million in fines from the Department of Health and Human Services (HHS).

Health organizations must prioritize security awareness and training, given the sensitive nature of the data they handle. Anthem's breach further illustrates the need for effective risk management strategies and oversight at all levels within healthcare organizations. Proactive engagement around compliance can prevent breaches and protect the sensitive information of millions, emphasizing that vigilance must be constant in cybersecurity endeavors.

The examination of these failures provides invaluable lessons that extend beyond individual organizations. They encompass the entire cybersecurity community, offering insights on strategies that can prevent similar missteps. Foremost, organizations must foster a culture of cybersecurity awareness, creating an environment where employees understand their role in upholding compliance. Regular training sessions, awareness campaigns, and open discussions can instill a sense of ownership and responsibility among employees. The implementation of a comprehensive cybersecurity training program can ensure that all employees recognize potential threats, understand compliance requirements, and respond appropriately to security incidents.

Moreover, organizations must establish a practice of rigorous security assessments and audits. Regular penetration testing, vulnerability scans, and third-party risk assessments are crucial for identifying weaknesses before they can be exploited. The emergence of a mindset focused on continuous improvement can significantly enhance an organization's security posture. Regulatory compliance is not just about adhering to rules; it is a journey that requires constant evaluation and adaptation to new threats.

Leadership engagement is also critical in promoting a culture of compliance. Executive buy-in ensures that cybersecurity measures are prioritized throughout the organization. Leaders must communicate the value of compliance, emphasizing its role in not only protecting the organization but also safeguarding customers and stakeholders. By integrating compliance into strategic planning and resource allocation, organizations can build resilient cybersecurity programs that adapt to the evolving threat landscape.

In conclusion, the stories of failure provide cautionary tales that resonate deeply within the cybersecurity landscape. The consequences of negligence can be severe, impacting both financial health and public trust. However, by learning from these missteps and adopting a proactive approach to compliance, organizations can navigate the turbulent waters of cybersecurity with greater success. Understanding the importance of vigilance, ensuring robust training, conducting regular assessments, and fostering a culture of accountability are essential steps on the path to compliance and security. As the adage goes, "Those who fail to learn from history are condemned to repeat it." In cybersecurity, there is no room for complacency; the price of inaction is far too steep.

Bridging the Gap: What We Can Learn

In the rapidly evolving realm of cybersecurity, organizations face a daily barrage of challenges, many of which can lead to significant repercussions if not handled adeptly. However, amidst these challenges lie invaluable lessons—stories of triumph and tales of failure that offer profound insights into the essence of cybersecurity compliance. By synthesizing these narratives, we can identify common themes and actionable takeaways that can guide organizations in their compliance journeys. As we explore these lessons, we will emphasize the importance of community and collaboration, highlighting how shared learning can bolster resilience in navigating the complex cybersecurity landscape.

In studying the success stories shared in the prior subchapter, a palpable sense of proactive engagement emerges as a common theme. Organizations that managed to successfully comply with cybersecurity regulations did so through a commitment to being ahead of the curve. They didn't wait for regulations to evolve; instead, they anticipated changes by investing in education and ongoing training. This underscores a crucial point for any organization: compliance should be viewed as an ongoing journey, not a one-time task. Continuous education fosters not only awareness but also a culture of compliance embedded within the organization.

For example, let's take the case of a global financial institution that embraced advanced training programs tailored to its employees at every level. Unlike many of their peers, who implemented compliance training strictly during onboarding, this institution conducted regular workshops, simulation exercises, and role-playing scenarios. The outcome? Employees were not just aware of compliance requirements; they were fully engaged with the implications of their daily actions and the resultant security posture of the business. By investing in their talent development, they cultivated a workforce that actively participated in identifying compliance gaps and suggesting measures to address them.

Similarly, the tales of failure illustrate a stark contrast, primarily characterized by complacency and a reactive approach to compliance. An example might be drawn from a healthcare provider that faced a stringent HIPAA fine after a substantial data breach. Their initial response was limited to a brief compliance audit prompted by the impending regulatory changes rather than a comprehensive evaluation of their systems. They learned, albeit the hard way, that neglecting to conduct regular audits and relying solely on past practices can lead to consequences that reverberate through their infrastructure. This incident reinforces the lesson that organizations should consistently revisit their security measures, aligning them with evolving regulations and industry best practices.

Moreover, the interplay between technology and human accountability underscores another recurring lesson. Success stories often feature organizations that integrated technology with human oversight. One such organization, a technology firm specializing in cloud services, adopted an automated compliance monitoring tool. However, they didn't rely only on this technology. An appointed compliance officer diligently reviewed alerts from the system, ensuring comprehensive oversight. This blend of automated and human-driven processes created a robust compliance framework that not only adhered to regulations but also established a trust factor among its clientele.

Conversely, a prominent retailer, which experienced a massive data breach, solely depended on automated systems for their security checks, largely bypassing the need for human intervention. The incident cost them not only their reputation but also significant financial resources in penalties and settlements. Their failure to recognize that technology alone cannot address every facet of compliance and security serves as a stark warning of the dangers of over-reliance on systems without human engagement. Organizations must aim for a harmonious balance where technology enhances compliance, but human judgment and accountability also play pivotal roles.

The synthesis of both success and failure narratives leads to another critical point: the essence of community and shared learning within the cybersecurity landscape. Organizations that actively engage with cybersecurity communities—whether through forums, industry conferences, or collaborative partnerships—have been able to enhance their compliance efforts significantly. The engagement fosters a culture of transparency and shared insights.

Let's consider an example from the energy sector, where a consortium of companies came together to address common cybersecurity challenges. Through regular collaboration sessions, they exchanged insights on compliance strategies that worked for them, analyzed cases of breaches that impacted their sector, and shared preventive measures. Collectively, they crafted a set of best practices that were subsequently adopted by all members. The result was a shared understanding of the regulatory landscape, leading to enhanced compliance visibility, mutual support, and a hop toward building a fortified defense against cyber threats.

This cooperative aspect cannot be overstated. In an age where cyber threats do not recognize boundaries, organizations cannot afford to operate in silos. The cybersecurity landscape is fundamentally multidisciplinary, incorporating legal, technological, psychological, and managerial elements. Thus, embracing a community-oriented approach not only fosters collaboration but enhances the collective intelligence of organizations navigating cybersecurity compliance, allowing them to stay ahead of emerging threats and changes in regulations.

Furthermore, reflecting on lessons learned should extend beyond the immediate compliance framework. Organizations must engage in post-mortem analyses of compliance failures and successes to identify applicable strategies for future enhancements. The act of reflection is pivotal, as it not only memorializes lessons learned but transforms them into operationalized strategies. For instance, a case study focused on a public-sector entity that faced major repercussions after its failure to comply with data protection laws illuminated the massive importance of internal audits. They adopted a practice of conducting regular internal evaluations and established time-bound plans for addressing any gaps identified through those evaluations. Transformative learning outcomes emerged, resulting in reinforced compliance protocols that aligned with both regulatory standards and organizational growth objectives.

In another striking instance, a technology startup that initially lacked a comprehensive compliance strategy faced an intense compliance audit just six months after launching its services. Through honest self-assessment, the founders recognized the need for a structured compliance framework. They embarked on a swift yet strategic pivot, fostering a compliance culture from the ground up. Their turnaround illustrated that a commitment to learning from both external standards and internal shortcomings could lead to a competitive advantage. Organizations can learn from these examples that mistakes do not need to result in stagnation; instead, they can catalyze transformative practices that enhance compliance positioning.

As organizations synthesize these lessons, a final essential takeaway emerges: the role of leadership in fostering a culture of compliance cannot be understated. Leaders set the tone for how compliance is perceived within an organization. They can influence the extent to which employees embrace compliance practices and encourage advocacy for community-based learning initiatives. Research shows that organizations with executive-level buy-in for compliance initiatives see a higher likelihood of adherence to regulatory requirements. This underscores the need for leaders to understand compliance not as a checklist but as an integral component of their organizational strategy.

Executive endorsements that promote compliance foster an atmosphere where employees feel empowered and responsible for compliance efforts. One success story featured the efforts of an executive at a leading telecommunications company who spearheaded a campaign that tied compliance initiatives directly to employee recognition programs. When employees were acknowledged for their contributions to compliance efforts, engagement surged, resulting in an organization-wide commitment to fostering security awareness among all ranks. The ripple effect of this recognition went beyond compliance; it fostered collective ownership of data security practices.

However, it is also important to acknowledge that challenges abound, and organizations must be equipped to pivot in response to new threats and changing regulations. The lessons gleaned from both successes and failures provide a framework for navigating these complexities, not just for individual organizations but for the broader ecosystem of businesses committed to cybersecurity compliance.

As we reflect on these lessons, organizations are called to action. Embrace ongoing education as a critical component of compliance, leverage both technology and human oversight, foster community collaboration, engage in continuous learning from successes and failures, and empower leadership to champion a culture of compliance within their ranks. These actionable insights pave the way for resilience in today's cybersecurity landscape, ensuring that organizations not only adapt to but thrive in this ever-changing environment.

In conclusion, bridging the gap between theoretical compliance frameworks and real-world implementation requires a genuine commitment to understanding and applying the lessons learned from both triumphs and challenges. By incorporating these lessons into daily operations and fostering collaborative relationships, organizations can equip themselves to navigate the evolving cybersecurity landscape effectively. The journey toward compliance is ongoing, but with the right strategies, insights, and community engagement, organizations can emerge as true guardians of the digital realm, protecting not just their interests but also the greater good. Sharing knowledge and nurturing a collective resilience will not only shape the future of individual organizations but also bolster the strength of the cybersecurity landscape as a whole.

Chapter 6: Ethical Considerations of Compliance

The Moral Imperative of Data Protection

In the digital age, where information flows freely and seamlessly across global networks, the ethical responsibilities of organizations in protecting sensitive data have come to the forefront of public discourse. With billions of data points being generated each day—from personal identifiers to financial records—the imperative to safeguard this information transcends mere compliance with regulatory requirements. It has evolved into a moral responsibility that organizations cannot afford to overlook. The principles of data protection are rooted in notions of privacy, rights, and respect, reflecting the societal expectations of trust that consumers place in businesses.

Historically, the concept of data privacy has its roots in the broader evolution of human rights. From the Magna Carta in 1215, which laid the groundwork for individual freedom, to the Universal Declaration of Human Rights in 1948, which codified the right to privacy as a fundamental human right, societal expectations have increasingly demanded that organizations treat individuals' personal data with dignity and care. These historical milestones have shaped the discourse on data protection, culminating in contemporary laws and regulations such as the General Data Protection Regulation (GDPR) in Europe and the California Consumer Privacy Act (CCPA) in the United States. However, compliance with these laws should not be viewed merely as a box to check; it is an essential step towards fulfilling a deeper ethical mandate.

To explore the moral imperative of data protection, we must first consider the psychological and emotional dimensions of data privacy. Individuals do not view their personal data as merely a collection of numbers or figures; they perceive it as an extension of themselves, imbued with personal significance and value. Each piece of data is intertwined with their identity, experiences, and aspirations. Therefore, when organizations mishandle, exploit, or inadequately protect this data, they infringe upon fundamental aspects of individuals' rights and sense of self-worth.

The ramifications of ethical breaches in data protection can be profound. Consider the case of a well-known retail giant that suffered a data breach in 2013. The incident involved the unauthorized access of over 40 million credit and debit card accounts, affecting customers who had entrusted the company with their sensitive information. The breach not only resulted in substantial financial losses for the organization but also compromised customer trust and loyalty. Affected individuals faced the threat of identity theft and financial fraud, leading to anxiety and emotional distress. As subsequent investigations revealed lapses in the retailer's data protection practices, it became clear that the breach was not merely a technical failure but a violation of trust—a breach of the ethical contract that existed between the organization and its customers.

This example is not isolated; it reflects a broader pattern where organizations have, at times, prioritized profit and growth over the fundamental rights of their customers. Such conduct raises poignant ethical questions: What is the value of customer trust? What are the long-term consequences of neglecting data protection as a core organizational priority? The ethical obligation to protect sensitive information transcends compliance; it entails a commitment to act with integrity, transparency, and accountability.

Engaging narratives illuminate these themes further. For instance, during the 2017 Equifax breach, the personal data of approximately 147 million Americans, ranging from Social Security numbers to addresses, was compromised. The fallout was tremendous, leading to widespread calls for greater accountability and reform in data protection practices. What stood out was the company's initial response to the breach, which was widely criticized as inadequate and dismissive. The delay in notifying affected individuals and the confusion surrounding the steps those individuals needed to take illustrated a profound misunderstanding of the moral responsibilities that accompany data stewardship.

Equifax's handling of the crisis was emblematic of a prevailing issue: too many organizations treat compliance as a legal obligation devoid of ethical considerations. In doing so, they risk prioritizing shareholder profits over societal good. Trust, once broken, is not easily repaired. Organizations that suffer data breaches may find their reputations tarnished, their customer bases diminished, and their market positions weakened.

Conversely, organizations that prioritize ethical data protection strategies reap long-term benefits. A notable example is the GDPR, which has set a gold standard for data protection practices across the globe. While the regulation has imposed strict compliance expectations on organizations, it has simultaneously fostered a culture of accountability and responsibility. Companies that embrace the principles of data protection not only enhance their compliance posture but also develop stronger relationships with their customers. Transparency in data handling, informed consent practices, and clear communication about data usage demonstrate a commitment to user trust and privacy, ethical imperatives that resonate deeply with consumers in today's digital landscape.

This underscores an important ethical principle: the notion of informed consent. When individuals share their personal information, they should do so with an understanding of how their data will be used and protected. Unfortunately, many organizations have fallen short in conveying this information, leading to a misalignment of expectations. A 2018 study revealed that while 79% of consumers expressed concern about their data privacy, only 5% felt they had complete control over their data. This disconnect reflects an ethical dilemma that businesses must urgently address. Organizations are not just custodians of data; they are also gatekeepers of trust. By reducing complex terms and conditions into simplified, accessible language, organizations can empower individuals to make informed decisions regarding their data, aligning ethical practices with business objectives.

As we navigate this intricate landscape, it is crucial to engage in self-reflection regarding our responsibilities, both as individuals and as custodians of sensitive information. Cybersecurity professionals, compliance officers, and organizational leaders must recognize that their ethical obligations extend beyond adhering to laws and regulations. They are stewards of data, responsible not only for compliance but also for cultivating an environment that values trust and respect.

This responsibility also extends to the broader organizational culture. A commitment to ethical data protection should permeate every level of the organization, driven by leadership that prioritizes data integrity. When organizations lack a transparent mindset and fail to foster an ethical culture, they risk creating a disconnect between their stated values and their actual behaviors. This misalignment can lead to complicity in ethical breaches, undermining the very fabric of trust that underpins customer relationships.

Training staff in ethical data handling practices plays an essential role in cultivating an informed workforce. Employees must grasp not only the technical aspects of data security but also the ethical ramifications of their actions. Organizations should conduct regular training sessions that emphasize the importance of integrity and ethical considerations in data handling. Real-world scenarios and case studies can serve as powerful teaching tools, allowing employees to appreciate the true impacts of their decisions.

Ethical responsibilities also extend beyond the walls of an organization. The interconnected nature of the digital landscape means that organizations must engage in collaborations that foster collective responsibility for data protection. Sharing best practices, participating in industry initiatives, and contributing to open dialog regarding ethical data stewardship can drive systemic change. By working collaboratively, organizations can elevate the standards for data protection and reshape public perceptions of trust in the digital realm.

Ultimately, the moral imperative of data protection necessitates that organizations not only comply with regulations but also embrace a broader ethical framework. Individuals deserve more than just compliance; they deserve respect, dignity, and protection. As organizations strive to navigate the complexities of data privacy, they must embrace this imperative as a guiding principle. This commitment will benefit not only individual organizations but society at large, fostering a digital ecosystem where trust and integrity can flourish.

In conclusion, as we deepen our understanding of the moral dimensions of cybersecurity, we must acknowledge that the ethical responsibilities of organizations in protecting sensitive information are not merely obligations—they are foundational tenets that uphold the integrity of the digital landscape. In choosing to prioritize ethical data practices alongside regulatory compliance, organizations position themselves as trusted stewards of sensitive information. This not only aligns with societal expectations but ultimately fortifies the relationships that organizations build with their customers. As guardians of the digital realm, the path forward demands a renewed commitment to ethical data protection—a commitment that recognizes and respects the humanity inherent in every data point we encounter.

Navigating Ethical Dilemmas

As cybersecurity continues to evolve and become more integral to our daily lives, professionals in the field frequently encounter ethical dilemmas that challenge their values, responsibilities, and the trust placed in them by clients and stakeholders. Balancing the competing demands of transparency, security, and compliance can often lead to challenging decisions. This subchapter delves into some of the most common ethical dilemmas faced by cybersecurity experts, using real-life examples to illustrate these complexities and providing insights from industry leaders and ethicists to guide decision-making.

One of the most significant ethical dilemmas faced by cybersecurity professionals is the tension between transparency and security. On one hand, stakeholders demand transparency regarding how organizations protect sensitive information and respond to incidents. On the other hand, disclosing too much information can create security vulnerabilities and expose organizations to additional risks. This dilemma often manifests in scenarios related to data breaches, vulnerability disclosures, and the sharing of threat intelligence.

Consider the case of a major data breach at a financial institution. After discovering that hackers had accessed sensitive customer data, the organization faced intense pressure to communicate the breach to its customers and the public. While transparency about the incident is crucial for maintaining trust and allowing customers to adjust their security practices, the organization also grappled with the possibility that revealing too many details could help the attackers exploit the vulnerability further. In this situation, cybersecurity professionals must navigate the fine line between being forthright with stakeholders and safeguarding the organization from potential fallout.

Another recurring ethical dilemma arises when organizations must disclose vulnerabilities identified in widely used software or hardware. When security researchers discover critical flaws, they face a moral and ethical challenge in deciding whether to disclose the vulnerability publicly or to provide the information exclusively to the vendor. Public disclosure can lead to rapid action and patching of the vulnerability, but can also put users at risk if a malicious actor exploits the information before a fix is available. In this example, ethical frameworks, such as the "responsible disclosure" approach, guide researchers to balance their obligations to the public and the software vendors.

The integration of artificial intelligence and machine learning in cybersecurity also introduces new ethical considerations. These technologies can enhance security capabilities, but they can also attack ethical boundaries, leading to biases in decision-making and unintended consequences. For instance, an AI-driven system may reject security requests based on flawed data analysis, potentially leading to legitimate users being unfairly classified as threats. Cybersecurity professionals must grapple with the consequences of relying on technology that may not align with their ethical standards and must actively work to minimize biases in AI algorithms to ensure fairness and efficacy.

In addition to these situations, cybersecurity professionals often face ethical decisions regarding monitoring employee activities to maintain security. With the increase in remote work and cloud-based systems, organizations are now equipped to monitor employees' online activities closely. However, navigating privacy concerns while ensuring organizational safety is a significant conflict. Monitoring tools can also infringe on employees' rights, stirring concern over constant surveillance. Ethical frameworks, such as the principle of proportionality—balancing security benefits with privacy intrusions—can help professionals determine appropriate levels of monitoring and communication with employees.

Another essential ethical consideration is the handling of sensitive data during incident response. For example, cybersecurity professionals responding to a ransomware attack may access confidential information to assess the severity of the attack. However, they must consider the ethical implications of how this data is handled and shared. Maintaining the confidentiality of customer data must remain a top priority, even in high-pressure situations. Cybersecurity leaders, therefore, need to devise strict protocols guiding the handling of sensitive information during incidents, ensuring they respect both ethical standards and legal obligations.

Insights from ethicists can provide valuable guidance in navigating these dilemmas. Dr. Helen Nissenbaum, a renowned ethicist in the field of privacy, emphasizes the importance of contextual integrity, which posits that ethical data practices must take into account the specific context in which information is shared. This concept shapes cybersecurity professionals' decisions regarding data use and disclosures, helping them evaluate whether actions align with both ethical and contextual expectations.

Furthermore, frameworks such as the Five Principles of Ethical Leadership can serve as a guide for cybersecurity professionals. These principles, known as the "Five P's"—Purpose, People, Process, Product, and Policy—encourage leaders to consider the implications of their decisions on various stakeholders, ensuring that their actions contribute to a more ethical cybersecurity landscape. For example, professionals should ensure that their cybersecurity practices account for the welfare of users while aligning with organizational goals.

To empower readers in navigating their ethical dilemmas, it is vital to provide practical strategies that help instill a decision-making framework. Engaging in ethical training and workshops can expose cybersecurity professionals to the ethical landscape within their organizations and from a broader perspective. Incorporating case studies and role-playing exercises in training sessions encourages them to analyze complex situations, fostering a culture of ethical reflection and discussion.

Establishing an open and collaborative environment for discussing ethical dilemmas within organizations is another critical strategy. Encouraging teams to share experiences and outcomes surrounding ethical decisions enables knowledge transfer and builds a community where ethical considerations are prioritized. Involving various stakeholders, including legal teams and business executives, increases accountability and fosters transparency throughout the decision-making process, ensuring varied perspectives are considered.

In addition to promoting a culture of open dialogue, organizations can create a “cybersecurity ethics committee” comprising members from different functions. This committee can offer guidance on ethical dilemmas, establish policies and procedures for handling sensitive issues, and serve as a hub for ongoing conversations about ethics in cybersecurity.

Not only does this provide a structured approach to ethical dilemmas, but it also reinforces accountability and fosters a collective commitment to ethical behavior.

Ultimately, navigating ethical dilemmas in cybersecurity requires professionals to be knowledgeable, reflective, and proactive in their approach. Keeping abreast of industry developments, engaging with ethical discussions, and practicing practical strategies can empower cybersecurity professionals to make informed decisions, enhance their ethical standing, and promote a culture of integrity within their organizations.

As the digital landscape continues to evolve, professionals must remain vigilant and adaptable in their decision-making. By honing their awareness of ethical dilemmas and embracing a robust ethical framework, cybersecurity practitioners can navigate the complexities of their roles with confidence, ensuring the digital realm remains secure while honoring the principles of transparency, trust, and human dignity.

The ethical challenges faced in cybersecurity are complex and multifaceted, demanding a nuanced approach to decision-making. By examining real-life scenarios, reflecting on ethical frameworks, and cultivating a proactive ethical culture within organizations, cybersecurity professionals can effectively navigate these dilemmas. In doing so, they uphold their commitment to protecting sensitive data and fostering an environment of transparency and accountability, ultimately enhancing the integrity of the cybersecurity profession as a whole.

The Role of Corporate Governance in Ethics

Corporate governance refers to the structures, policies, and processes through which organizations are directed and controlled. It encompasses the mechanisms by which stakeholders—including shareholders, management, and the board of directors—interact and make decisions about the direction, risk management, and stewardship of the organization. In the context of ethics, effective corporate governance not only strives to align the interests of diverse stakeholders but also establishes a framework where ethical conduct is prioritized and integrated into the organization's culture.

To understand the role of corporate governance in ethics, it is essential to recognize that ethical behavior within organizations is not merely a product of personal morality or individual decisions. Rather, it is heavily influenced by the organizational environment and structures that govern behavior. When leaders set high ethical standards and cultivate a culture of accountability and transparency, organizations are more likely to foster compliance and ethical conduct among employees, ultimately reinforcing stakeholder trust and enhancing their corporate reputation.

One illustrative case is that of Johnson & Johnson, whose governance structure emphasizes ethical principles through its Credo. This guiding document articulates the company’s responsibilities to various stakeholders, including customers, employees, communities, and shareholders. The Credo serves not only as a moral compass for decision-making but also shapes the company's governance framework by emphasizing ethical behavior as foundational to long-term success.

In 1982, when seven people died after taking Tylenol capsules tainted with cyanide, Johnson & Johnson's leadership faced a pivotal moment that tested their ethical commitments. The company swiftly recalled over 31 million bottles of Tylenol, prioritizing consumer safety over short-term financial loss. This decision, driven by the guidance of their Credo, reinforced the perception that ethical governance is more than just an administrative function; it is vital for protecting the interests of all stakeholders. The proactive steps taken by Johnson & Johnson in crisis management emphasized how a strong ethical framework within corporate governance could make a substantial difference in navigating potential pitfalls.

Moreover, corporate governance structures serve as scaffolding to bolster ethical practices through mechanisms such as codes of conduct, ethics training programs, and compliance oversight. For instance, large corporations often employ chief compliance officers who report directly to the board of directors, creating pathways for ethical concerns to be raised without fear of retaliation. Such roles are critical in conveying that ethical conduct is a priority at the highest levels of the organization.

A compelling example comes from Enron, a case that starkly stands in contrast to Johnson & Johnson. Once heralded as a leader in corporate governance, Enron collapsed in 2001 due to widespread accounting fraud driven by a corporate culture that prioritized profit over ethics. The company's governance structure failed to establish a framework that actively encouraged ethical behavior. When executives engaged in deceptive practices, they received no adequate checks or balances, ultimately resulting in a catastrophic loss of employee jobs and investor savings. This highlights the risk organizations face when ethical considerations are neglected in governance and demonstrates the crucial need for a robust ethical framework.

Effective corporate governance also necessitates accountability, which serves to ensure that ethical standards are enforced and not merely aspirational. Organizations that adopt transparency initiatives, such as regular reporting on ethical compliance and governance checks, better position themselves to identify ethical breaches and address them expediently. Starbucks is a prime example in this regard. The company has long championed responsible sourcing and sustainability initiatives, creating a transparent supply chain framework as part of its governance efforts. By publicly reporting on their ethical practices, they invite scrutiny and hold themselves accountable to stakeholders, reinforcing their commitment to ethical governance.

Leadership plays a crucial role in fostering an ethical culture within corporate governance. The tone at the top significantly influences an organization's ethical climate, and leaders must exhibit the behaviors they wish to see across the organization. Effective leaders—those who model ethical decision-making and create an environment where employees feel safe to express ethical considerations—are instrumental in embedding ethics into the governance framework. Leadership training programs that emphasize ethical leadership can shape those in managerial positions to prioritize ethics in their decision-making.

One notable success story is that of Unilever, which has embedded sustainable business practices through its Sustainable Living Plan. The company's CEO has taken a public stance on sustainability and corporate responsibility, which permeates their governance practices. By directly correlating ethical behavior with long-term value creation in their strategic objectives, Unilever has cultivated an organizational culture that values responsibility and integrity. This approach is critical as it demonstrates that ethical governance not only mitigates risks but can also provide a competitive advantage and drive growth.

To further reinforce the significance of corporate governance in ethics, the mechanisms of internal and external audits deserve attention. Regular audits serve as checks on compliance with ethical standards, while external assessments can provide unbiased evaluations of an organization's ethical practices. The integration of audits in governance frameworks encourages organizations to continually improve their ethical practices and to respond proactively to areas of deficiency. Companies that engage in routine evaluations of their ethical conduct and governance structures are often better positioned to meet compliance standards and address risks effectively.

The importance of stakeholder engagement in corporate governance cannot be overlooked. By actively involving stakeholders in decision-making and governance processes, organizations can better understand ethical concerns and expectations. This engagement demonstrates a respect for diverse perspectives and reinforces ethical behavior as an organizational priority. For instance, many companies are now establishing advisory boards that include external stakeholders, allowing them to provide insights on ethical considerations related to governance. These collaborations can enhance accountability and strengthen ethical practices, ultimately enhancing stakeholder trust.

Ethical governance is also closely tied to corporate social responsibility (CSR). Organizations that prioritize ethics often extend their ethical considerations beyond compliance with regulations toward broader societal responsibilities. This shift not only helps mitigate potential risks and legal repercussions but can also generate goodwill among consumers and foster loyalty. Patagonia is often cited as a leader in integrating CSR into its governance structure, demonstrating a commitment to environmental sustainability and ethical labor practices. The company's emphasis on ethical governance has not only elevated its brand image but has also attracted consumers who value corporate responsibility.

In conclusion, the role of corporate governance in ethics is multifaceted and critical for the success of organizations in today's dynamic marketplace. By establishing governance structures that prioritize ethical behavior, organizations can create a culture of accountability and transparency that supports compliance while reinforcing core ethical values. Leadership commitment is essential for embedding these ethical standards into everyday decision-making, ensuring that ethics anchors corporate strategies rather than being relegated to compliance checklists.

As readers consider the role of corporate governance in shaping ethical behavior, they are encouraged to reflect on their organizations' governance frameworks and advocate for practices that promote ethical standards. As stakeholders, they can influence their own corporate environments, emphasizing that compliance transcends mere adherence to rules—it embodies a commitment to doing what is right. By actively participating in the development and promotion of ethical governance, readers can aspire to be guardians of the digital realm, navigating the complexities of compliance with integrity and purpose.

Chapter 7: Future Trends in Cybersecurity

Emerging Technologies and Their Impact

As organizations increasingly find themselves in the crosshairs of cyber threats, the rapid evolution of technology presents both remarkable opportunities and daunting challenges in the cybersecurity landscape. Emerging technologies such as artificial intelligence (AI), machine learning (ML), and blockchain are reshaping how organizations protect their digital assets, manage risks, and enhance compliance with regulatory frameworks. This subchapter delves into how these innovations not only fortify defenses but also introduce complex considerations that organizations must navigate as they strive for both security and compliance.

Artificial Intelligence in Cybersecurity

Artificial intelligence, with its ability to analyze vast amounts of data and learn from patterns, has become a transformative force in the realm of cybersecurity. AI systems can process and analyze enormous volumes of logs, transactions, and network traffic far more efficiently than human analysts. This capability is crucial in a world where cybercriminals exploit vulnerabilities at an increasingly rapid pace.

Organizations such as Darktrace have pioneered the use of AI in detecting and responding to cyber threats in real time.

Darktrace's AI platform, known as the Enterprise Immune System, operates much like the human immune system. It learns what constitutes normal behavior in a network, enabling it to identify anomalies that may indicate a breach or malicious activity. By using unsupervised learning techniques, AI can adapt to new threats without needing pre-programmed responses, providing a dynamic defense mechanism that evolves alongside the threat landscape.

The benefits of AI in cybersecurity are substantial. Automated threat detection reduces the time between breach and response, enabling organizations to actuate defensive measures promptly. Moreover, AI-driven analytics can enhance the accuracy of threat identification, minimizing false positives that often burden security teams.

However, while AI offers significant advantages, it is not without risks. The very capabilities that make AI powerful can also be exploited by cybercriminals. As organizations invest in AI for defense, adversaries are also developing AI tools to launch sophisticated attacks, further escalating the arms race in cybersecurity. Furthermore, the reliance on AI can lead to overconfidence in automated systems, resulting in potential blind spots if human analysts fail to remain engaged with the evolving threat landscape.

Machine Learning as a Cybersecurity Enhancement

Machine learning, a subset of AI that focuses on the development of algorithms that allow systems to learn from data, is proving to be equally transformative in cybersecurity. The ability of machine learning algorithms to recognize complex patterns in datasets can be leveraged for numerous cybersecurity applications, from user behavior analytics to the detection of malware.

Take, for instance, the way machine learning is employed by security vendor CrowdStrike. Their Falcon platform utilizes machine learning to gather and analyze telemetry from endpoints across client networks. By continuously learning from the data it collects, Falcon can identify malicious content and adversarial techniques, enhancing its threat detection capabilities exponentially. This proactive approach allows organizations to not only react to threats but also predict and preempt them based on behavioral patterns.

Moreover, machine learning's application in anomaly detection can unveil sophisticated attacks such as advanced persistent threats (APTs), which are designed to remain undetected for extended periods. Traditional security measures may overlook subtle signs of compromise, but with the insight provided by machine learning, organizations are better equipped to identify threats that evade conventional detection methods.

Yet, the integration of machine learning into cybersecurity also comes with its hurdles. The effectiveness of machine learning models heavily relies on the quality and diversity of training data. If the data used to train algorithms is biased or incomplete, it can lead to inaccurate threat detection and increased vulnerability. Organizations must address these challenges by continuously updating their datasets and refining their models to adapt to new attack vectors.

Blockchain Technology's Role in Cybersecurity

Blockchain technology, initially developed as the foundation for cryptocurrencies, has emerged as a powerful tool for enhancing cybersecurity, particularly in areas such as secure data sharing and identity management. The decentralized and immutable nature of blockchain means that once data is recorded, it cannot be altered or tampered with, making it a reliable solution for safeguarding sensitive information.

In a practical application of blockchain for cybersecurity, IBM has engaged with enterprises to implement blockchain solutions that enhance data integrity and security. By utilizing a shared ledger, organizations can track transactions and data exchanges in real time, significantly reducing the risk of unauthorized access and data manipulation.

Another compelling application of blockchain in cybersecurity is in identity management. The traditional model of centralized identity management is often fraught with vulnerabilities, as a single breach can compromise an entire database of user credentials. By employing a decentralized approach through blockchain, organizations can empower users to control their own identities, leveraging cryptographic keys for secure authentication without relying on a central authority that can be exploited.

However, while blockchain holds significant promise, it is essential to recognize that it is not a silver bullet. Implementing blockchain solutions necessitates a robust understanding of its architecture and potential vulnerabilities. Without proper implementation and governance, organizations may inadvertently expose themselves to security risks.

Navigating Compliance with Emerging Technologies

As organizations embrace emerging technologies, the relationship between cybersecurity and compliance becomes increasingly intricate. Regulatory frameworks such as the General Data Protection Regulation (GDPR) and the Health Insurance Portability and Accountability Act (HIPAA) impose rigorous standards on how organizations manage and protect sensitive data. The intersection of cybersecurity and compliance mandates that businesses not only employ cutting-edge technologies but also ensure that their practices align with regulatory expectations.

For instance, the algorithms used in AI and machine learning must be transparent and explainable, especially when handling personal data. This raises significant challenges related to compliance; organizations must be prepared to justify their use of these technologies and demonstrate that they do not inadvertently violate users' rights.

Moreover, the implementation of blockchain to secure personal data is subject to interpretation under various regulatory frameworks. While blockchain's immutability can enhance data integrity, it may also present challenges related to data erasure and data subjects' rights, particularly under regulations like the GDPR, which entitles individuals to request the deletion of their data. Organizations must reconcile the advantages offered by blockchain technology with compliance requirements that prioritize user control and privacy.

Harnessing Innovation for Enhanced Security

To thrive in this shifting landscape, organizations must view emerging technologies as integral components of their cybersecurity strategy rather than isolated solutions. Embracing a holistic approach allows businesses to leverage the strengths of AI, ML, and blockchain while addressing their vulnerabilities.

To this end, organizations should invest in training their cybersecurity teams to better understand and utilize these technologies. By fostering a culture of learning and adaptability, businesses can empower their personnel to take full advantage of innovative tools, rather than relying solely on outdated methodologies. As the cybersecurity landscape continues to evolve, organizations must remain vigilant and proactive, adapting their strategies and practices to address new threats.

Moreover, collaboration with technology partners and cybersecurity vendors can offer organizations valuable insights into the effective implementation of emerging technologies. By engaging with experts in the field, organizations can gain access to cutting-edge solutions and best practices that enhance their overall security posture.

Real-World Applications and Case Studies

As organizations worldwide adopt emerging technologies, numerous success stories illustrate the tangible benefits they can yield. The financial services sector, often a prime target for cybercriminals, has embraced AI and machine learning to revolutionize its security practices.

For example, Wells Fargo has utilized AI-driven risk assessment tools to detect potential fraudulent activities. By analyzing patterns of transactional behavior and developing risk profiles, Wells Fargo is better equipped to flag suspicious activities before they escalate into major breaches. Such proactive measures not only mitigate risks but also reinforce compliance with stringent financial regulatory requirements.

In the public sector, the City of Tallinn, Estonia, has established itself as a leader in cybersecurity through the use of blockchain technology. The Estonian government leverages blockchain to secure public records, enhance e-governance, and provide citizens with more control over their personal data. This innovative approach has not only fortified the country's defenses against cyber threats but has also fostered trust among residents regarding the handling of sensitive information.

The retail sector presents another compelling case for emerging technologies. Target, after suffering a significant data breach in 2013, has made substantial investments in AI and machine learning to revamp its cybersecurity framework. The company's commitment to implementing real-time analytics and advanced threat detection has transformed its security posture, enabling it to respond swiftly to emerging threats and maintain compliance with industry regulations.

Conclusion

The dynamic landscape of cybersecurity is shaped by the relentless advance of technology, creating an environment where organizations must innovate or risk obsolescence. Artificial intelligence, machine learning, and blockchain hold immense potential for enhancing security defenses, but they also introduce new complexities that demand careful navigation.

As organizations adapt to these emerging technologies, a multifaceted approach that combines technical innovation with compliance awareness is essential. By leveraging the power of AI for threat detection, deploying machine learning for behavioral analysis, and embracing blockchain for secure data management, businesses can forge a comprehensive cybersecurity strategy that not only protects their digital assets but also meets evolving regulatory demands.

The journey towards integrating these technologies is not without challenges, but forward-thinking organizations that remain committed to continuous improvement and learning will find themselves better equipped to face the ever-evolving landscape of cyber threats. By harnessing the potential of emerging technologies while prioritizing compliance, organizations can emerge as true guardians of the digital realm, ensuring the security and integrity of their operations in an increasingly complex cyber environment.

The Evolution of Cyber Threats

In the rapidly shifting landscape of cybersecurity, the nature of cyber threats has undergone significant evolution over recent years. As organizations bolster their defenses with advanced technologies and security protocols, cyberattackers are responding not only with creativity but also with increasing sophistication. This subchapter delves into this perpetual game of cat and mouse, illustrating how emerging technologies, ever-adaptive tactics, and new vulnerabilities intertwine to create a complex threat environment.

At the forefront of contemporary cyber threats is the rise of ransomware, a particularly insidious form of malware that has wreaked havoc across various sectors. Ransomware attacks involve encrypting a victim's data, rendering it inaccessible until a ransom is paid to the attacker. Notably, over the last few years, ransomware has transformed into a multimillion-dollar industry, with attackers using a range of strategies to maximize their financial gains.

A striking example of ransomware's evolution is the notorious Colonial Pipeline attack in May 2021, which forced the shutdown of a major fuel pipeline serving the Eastern United States. Attackers employed a ransomware strain known as DarkSide, which not only targeted the organization but also created panic and disruption across the broader economy. The incident exemplified how ransomware has shifted from targeting individual businesses to causing widespread societal impacts. The attackers, anticipating the urgency with which companies would need to restore operations, demanded a ransom of approximately $4.4 million, which the company paid in a bid to quickly regain access to crucial operational data. Colonial Pipeline's experience reveals the potency of ransomware and highlights the significant risks organizations face when they fall prey to these assaults.

As ransomware continues to evolve, cybercriminals are increasingly incorporating double extortion tactics. After encrypting data for ransom, attackers threaten to publish sensitive information online, thus escalating pressure on victims to comply. This strategy was infamously employed by the REvil group, which targeted the meat processing giant JBS in June 2021. Faced with the prospect of public exposure of sensitive data, JBS opted to pay $11 million to ensure that the data would not see the light of day. Such incidents underscore how the dual threat of data loss and reputational damage pressures organizations into compliance, ultimately facilitating a more lucrative business for cybercriminals.

Another cyber threat on the rise is the exploitation of the Internet of Things (IoT) devices. The proliferation of IoT devices—ranging from smart thermostats and home security systems to industrial sensors—has increased the attack surface available to cybercriminals. Many of these devices are equipped with minimal security features or are left with default passwords, making them easy targets for attackers.

A striking case study is the 2016 Mirai botnet attack, where hackers exploited IoT devices to create a massive network of compromised systems. These systems, predominantly consumer products like cameras and routers, were hijacked to launch a distributed denial-of-service (DDoS) attack against Dyn, a major DNS provider. The attack resulted in widespread internet outages, affecting millions of users and disrupting access to major websites, including Netflix, Twitter, and Reddit. The Mirai botnet represents a critical inflection point in understanding the vulnerabilities posed by IoT devices and serves as a chilling reminder of the potential damage that can be inflicted through seemingly innocuous gadgets.

As the landscape of cyber threats continues to expand and evolve, the need for proactive threat detection and mitigation strategies becomes paramount. Organizations cannot solely rely on traditional security measures; they must integrate advanced analytics and AI-driven technologies into their defense strategies to stay ahead of evolving threats. Leveraging machine learning algorithms enables organizations to detect anomalies in network traffic, identifying potential threats before they can inflict harm. By proactively monitoring user behavior and system alterations, organizations can enhance their cybersecurity posture and respond swiftly to potential breaches.

For instance, security information and event management (SIEM) systems have become indispensable tools for organizations aiming to fortify their defenses. These systems aggregate and analyze data from various sources, providing a holistic view of organizational security. By centralizing threat intelligence, SIEM solutions can identify patterns and detect irregularities that may indicate a security breach. When coupled with advanced machine learning, these systems can continuously adapt and improve, honing their accuracy over time.

Beyond technological solutions, fostering a culture of security awareness among employees is crucial for effective cybersecurity. Phishing attacks—where attackers impersonate legitimate entities to trick individuals into revealing sensitive information—remain one of the most prevalent tactics employed by cybercriminals. A comprehensive cybersecurity training program can empower employees to recognize these attacks, significantly reducing the likelihood of successful breaches. Organizations should conduct regular training sessions, simulate phishing scenarios, and reinforce best practices to cultivate vigilant and informed employees who can act as the first line of defense against cyber threats.

Moreover, organizations should adopt the principle of 'assume breach' as part of their cybersecurity strategy. This proactive mindset acknowledges that, despite preventive measures, breaches can and will occur. By preparing for such incidents through detailed incident response planning, organizations can minimize the impact of an attack. This includes creating cross-functional response teams that can swiftly engage in containment, investigation, and remediation efforts once a breach is detected.

Equally critical is the implementation of multi-factor authentication (MFA), a simple yet effective tactic to provide an additional layer of security. MFA requires users to provide multiple forms of verification to access systems, significantly reducing the odds of unauthorized access, even if a password is compromised. As password reuse remains a common pitfall for many users, implementing MFA acts as a formidable barrier against would-be attackers.

Another area warranting attention is the evolving threat landscape posed by state-sponsored actors. Nation-state cyber operations have gained considerable traction, often blurring the boundaries between cybercrime and geopolitical motivation. Intelligence reports indicate that these actors engage in sophisticated espionage, infrastructure sabotage, and disinformation campaigns to achieve strategic objectives. An example is the SolarWinds cyberattack of

2020, attributed to Russian state-sponsored hackers who exploited vulnerabilities in software widely used by U.S. government agencies and corporate networks. The attackers were able to remain undetected for months, gaining access to sensitive information that had significant ramifications on national security and corporate governance.

As the distinction between traditional cyber threats and state-sponsored activities continues to blur, organizations must adopt a more comprehensive threat intelligence-sharing approach. Collaborative networks that facilitate the sharing of information on emerging threats can enable organizations to adapt more effectively in real time. Security threats may affect numerous sectors simultaneously, and while a specific organization may be attacked directly, others can fortify their defenses based on shared intelligence.

In addressing the evolving nature of cyber threats, organizations must also consider the implications of regulatory compliance and how to balance compliance requirements with the agility needed to respond to emerging threats. As governments ramp up legislation around data protection and cyber hygiene, organizations face the dual challenge of implementing controls that not only satisfy compliance demands but also dynamically align with evolving threat landscapes.

To navigate this complexity, organizations should consider adopting agile compliance frameworks that allow them to assess risks and implement changes continuously. By aligning cybersecurity initiatives with compliance requirements, organizations can simultaneously satisfy regulatory expectations while fortifying defenses against evolving threats.

Ultimately, understanding the evolution of cyber threats is vital for organizations seeking to protect their assets and maintain trust with stakeholders. The adaptation of attackers' tactics, emerging vulnerabilities from new technologies such as IoT, and the continued onslaught of ransomware require organizations to remain vigilant and proactive. By fostering a culture of cybersecurity awareness, leveraging advanced threat detection technologies, embracing shared intelligence, and adopting agile compliance frameworks, organizations can not only enhance their cybersecurity posture but also thrive in an increasingly complex digital environment.

In conclusion, as we look to the future, it is evident that the threat landscape will continue to evolve. Cybersecurity is not a destination but a continuous journey of adaptation and innovation. Organizations that proactively address the evolving nature of threats, foster collaboration, and embrace technological advancements can position themselves as "Guardians of the Digital Realm." The stakes are high, but with preparedness, resilience, and a commitment to continuous improvement, organizations can navigate the tumultuous waters of cybersecurity and emerge stronger than before.

Preparing for a Cyber Future

In a rapidly evolving digital landscape, cybersecurity compliance is not a static target but rather a dynamic journey that organizations must navigate with foresight and agility. As technology continues to advance at an unprecedented pace, the strategies and frameworks that once ensured security and compliance may become obsolete overnight. It is essential for organizations to embrace a forward-looking perspective that recognizes the inevitability of change and prepares them for the unknown challenges that lie ahead.

The cybersecurity landscape is influenced by myriad factors, including technological advancements, regulatory shifts, and social dynamics. As cyber threats become more sophisticated and attacks increase in frequency, compliance requirements will evolve to address new risks and vulnerabilities. Experts predict that the future of cybersecurity compliance will see an intensified focus on proactive measures rather than reactive responses. Organizations will need to cultivate a mindset that encourages continuous adaptation and learning, empowering their teams to stay ahead of the curve.

One of the most significant trends anticipated in the realm of cybersecurity compliance is the increasing regulatory scrutiny on businesses. Governments worldwide are expected to enact more stringent regulations that hold organizations accountable for data protection. The European Union's General Data Protection Regulation (GDPR) has set a precedent that many other jurisdictions are beginning to follow. Companies operating internationally will need to navigate a patchwork of regulations, each with its own compliance mandates. This reality will necessitate the development of flexible compliance frameworks that can quickly adapt to changes in laws and standards.

Regulatory bodies are likely to enhance their capabilities for monitoring compliance. With the rise of data analytics and machine learning, regulators may increasingly employ these technologies to conduct more comprehensive audits and inspections. Organizations must be prepared to demonstrate their adherence to regulatory standards through detailed documentation and transparent reporting practices. This shift underscores the importance of investing in compliance technologies that streamline data management and facilitate timely reporting.

In tandem with evolving regulations, the skills required of cybersecurity professionals will also transform. As cyber threats grow in complexity, so too must the expertise of those tasked with defending against them. Organizations will need professionals proficient not only in technical skills but also in understanding the business implications of cybersecurity. Experts predict that demand will rise for individuals who possess a combination of technical acumen, strategic thinking, and leadership qualities.

Soft skills such as communication, collaboration, and empathy will become increasingly valuable in cybersecurity roles. As organizations strive to foster a security-first culture, professionals who can articulate the importance of compliance and influence stakeholders will be essential for success. The ability to translate complex technical concepts into language that resonates with non-technical stakeholders—and vice versa—will enable cybersecurity leaders to bridge the gap between IT and business operations effectively.

Moreover, an emphasis on continuous learning will be critical for cybersecurity professionals. The landscape of threats and technologies is constantly shifting, necessitating a commitment to lifelong education. Organizations should prioritize upskilling programs that enable employees to stay abreast of the latest trends, tools, and best practices in cybersecurity. These initiatives could take the form of workshops, certifications, and collaborative learning opportunities. By investing in their workforce development, organizations will not only strengthen their compliance posture but also enhance overall employee engagement and satisfaction.

As organizations lay the groundwork for future compliance, fostering a culture of innovation and resilience will be essential. This culture must permeate every level of the organization, from the executive suite to individual team members. Leaders play a crucial role in creating an environment where experimentation and new ideas are encouraged. Organizations should embrace a mindset that views challenges as opportunities for growth, rather than obstacles to be avoided.

To achieve this, organizations can implement practices such as regular brainstorming sessions, innovation labs, and cross-functional collaboration initiatives. By breaking down silos and promoting open communication, teams can harness collective intelligence to develop creative solutions to emerging compliance challenges. Additionally, rewarding and recognizing innovative thinking can incentivize employees to contribute their ideas and insights, fostering a culture of proactive problem-solving.

Technology will undoubtedly play a pivotal role in shaping the future of cybersecurity compliance. Emerging technologies, including artificial intelligence (AI), machine learning, and blockchain, present both opportunities and challenges. Harnessing AI technologies can enhance threat detection capabilities and enable organizations to automate compliance processes, reducing the risk of human error. However, the ethical implications of these technologies must be carefully considered. Organizations must prioritize responsible AI practices to ensure that compliance strategies do not inadvertently harm privacy or security.

Blockchain technology, with its decentralized and immutable nature, has the potential to revolutionize data protection and compliance. By leveraging blockchain for secure record-keeping and transparent auditing, organizations can enhance their accountability and reduce the risk of data breaches. As interest in blockchain grows, cybersecurity professionals will need to develop expertise in this technology to ensure compliance in blockchain-based environments.

As organizations look to the horizon, they must also remain vigilant about emerging threats. The evolution of cyberattacks will demand proactive, adaptive security postures. Ransomware, for instance, has become a leading concern, and attackers are continually refining their tactics. Organizations must prepare for the possibility of state-sponsored attacks and the exploitation of new technologies, such as the Internet of Things (IoT) and 5G networks. A robust incident response plan, coupled with threat intelligence, will be indispensable for effectively countering such threats.

Discussions regarding privacy and cybersecurity will also shape the narrative moving forward. As consumers become increasingly aware of their data rights, organizations will face mounting pressure to prioritize transparency and ethical practices. Compliance will no longer be viewed solely as a regulatory obligation; it will also be a fundamental aspect of building trust with customers and stakeholders.

Forward-thinking organizations will view compliance as an integral part of their brand identity and customer experience strategy. Engaging consumers in conversations about data protection and privacy will enhance their confidence and loyalty. Regular communication about compliance efforts, policies, and updates will be key to cultivating a positive relationship with customers.

As the cybersecurity landscape continues to evolve, businesses must recognize the value of collaboration and knowledge-sharing. Cybersecurity is not solely the responsibility of the IT department; it is a shared accountability that extends across the entire organization. Creating forums for collaboration, both internally and with external partners, will allow organizations to leverage diverse perspectives and experiences to address compliance challenges.

Public-private partnerships can facilitate knowledge exchange and proactive threat sharing. Organizations should collaborate with government agencies, industry partners, and academic institutions to develop best practices and respond to emerging threats. By working together, stakeholders can foster a more resilient cybersecurity ecosystem and enhance compliance efforts across sectors.

In the face of these emerging trends, resilience will be a defining characteristic of successful organizations. Resilience refers to the ability to withstand and recover from adverse events while continuing to innovate and adapt. Developing a resilient compliance framework involves not only preparing for potential risks but also embracing the possibility of failure as a stepping stone toward progress.

Organizations should invest in continuous monitoring and risk assessment to anticipate potential vulnerabilities and proactively address them. Leveraging data analytics to assess the effectiveness of compliance efforts can provide valuable insights that inform future strategies. This iterative approach ensures that compliance remains adaptive, relevant, and aligned with the organization's goals.

In conclusion, preparing for a cyber future requires organizations to adopt a mindset of continuous adaptation and learning. The landscape of cybersecurity compliance is poised to evolve dramatically, driven by regulatory changes, emerging technologies, and shifting consumer expectations. Organizations must cultivate a culture of innovation and resilience, engaging their teams in proactive problem-solving and collaboration. By investing in the development of cybersecurity professionals and fostering a commitment to responsible practices, organizations can position themselves for success in an increasingly complex digital world. As they embrace the challenges and opportunities that lie ahead, the guardians of the digital realm will be better equipped to navigate the turbulent waters of cybersecurity compliance.

Chapter 8: Guardians in Action: Emerging Technologies

Innovations in Cybersecurity Tools

In the rapidly evolving landscape of cybersecurity, the tools and technologies utilized by organizations are becoming increasingly sophisticated. This transformation is not only a response to the growing number of cyber threats but also a proactive measure to ensure compliance with regulatory standards. As businesses contend with the complexities of protecting sensitive data, a new generation of cybersecurity tools is surfacing—innovative solutions that leverage automation, artificial intelligence (AI), and advanced encryption to fortify defenses and streamline compliance efforts. This subchapter will explore several of these innovations, illustrating their impact through real-world examples and case studies, ultimately demonstrating how organizations can harness these advancements to enhance their cybersecurity capabilities.

One of the most significant advancements in the realm of cybersecurity compliance is the rise of automated compliance solutions. These tools leverage automation to simplify, accelerate, and enhance the compliance process, reducing the burden on organizations and enabling them to focus on their core operations. Traditional compliance management often involves repetitive manual processes, which can be time-consuming and prone to human error. Automated solutions aim to eliminate these challenges by streamlining workflows and providing real-time visibility into compliance status.

For example, let's consider a pharmaceutical company that must adhere to stringent regulations like the Health Insurance Portability and Accountability Act (HIPAA) and the Food and Drug Administration (FDA) data integrity requirements. Prior to implementing an automated compliance solution, the organization faced significant challenges in maintaining its compliance status due to the manual tracking of various regulatory requirements. The compliance team would spend countless hours sifting through documents, spreadsheets, and outdated practices to ensure all measures were met, leading to delays and potential risks of non-compliance.

After adopting an automated compliance management tool, the company transformed its compliance efforts. The new solution combined policy management, risk assessment, and audit management into a single platform. By automating workflows, the organization achieved not only an impressive reduction in time spent on compliance documentation but also enhanced accuracy and reliability in compliance reporting. Moreover, the integration of real-time alerts and notifications ensured that key stakeholders remained informed of any changes in regulations or compliance statuses, empowering them to act promptly and efficiently.

This success story illustrates the significant advantages that automated compliance solutions provide. Organizations can maximize their efficiency while minimizing risks, ultimately leading to better regulatory adherence and a stronger overall security posture.

Another groundbreaking area in cybersecurity is the development of threat intelligence platforms (TIPs). Cyber threats are becoming increasingly sophisticated and targeted, making it crucial for organizations to stay ahead of the curve. TIPs serve as centralized systems that aggregate, analyze, and share threat intelligence data from multiple sources, enabling organizations to recognize and respond to emerging threats more effectively.

For instance, a financial services firm recently faced multiple cyber-attack attempts that aimed to exploit vulnerabilities in its systems. The organization understood that to protect itself effectively, it needed to rely on actionable intelligence derived from a wealth of threat data. After implementing a threat intelligence platform, the company began to aggregate data from various sources, including internal asset logs, external threat feeds, and information shared by industry peers. This centralized intelligence gathering allowed the organization to see patterns and correlations that would have been nearly impossible to detect manually.

With this enhanced visibility, the financial firm was able to identify and block attacks before they could even impact their systems. The TIP not only provided the security team with actionable insights but also facilitated collaboration with other financial institutions, allowing them to collectively share intelligence about threats and attack methodologies. As a result, the organization saw a significant decrease in successful cyberattacks and improved overall security resilience.

The benefits of employing a threat intelligence platform extend beyond mere defense mechanisms. By staying informed about the latest attack vectors and trends, organizations can better inform their compliance strategies. Understanding the potential risks they face enables organizations to allocate resources more effectively, ensuring that their compliance measures align with their actual threat landscape.

Advanced encryption methods represent yet another critical innovation in the field of cybersecurity compliance. With the exponential growth of data and the shift toward cloud storage solutions, organizations are tasked with protecting sensitive information in increasingly complex environments. Traditional encryption methods, while effective, are often not enough to mitigate the risks associated with advanced threats. In this regard, new encryption technologies are emerging to provide organizations with more robust data protection options.

One notable innovation is homomorphic encryption, a method that allows computations to be performed on encrypted data without needing to decrypt it first. This groundbreaking approach enables organizations to utilize cloud-based services while safeguarding sensitive data, ensuring that compliance with regulations such as GDPR and HIPAA is upheld. A tech startup that handles sensitive consumer data adopted homomorphic encryption as part of its data protection strategy. This implementation allowed the company to process and analyze encrypted data while securely maintaining compliance with privacy regulations.

By utilizing this innovative encryption method, the startup gained a competitive edge in the market, positioning itself as a leader in data protection and privacy compliance. The ability to leverage cloud resources without compromising data security enabled them to innovate and grow rapidly, all while meeting the stringent regulatory requirements applicable to their industry.

As cyber threats continue to evolve, organizations must remain vigilant and proactive in their cybersecurity efforts. Implementing innovative cybersecurity tools is one of the most effective ways to enhance compliance and protect sensitive information from malicious actors. These tools not only offer practical solutions but also empower organizations to adapt to changing regulatory demands.

In addition to the advancements mentioned, machine learning (ML) and artificial intelligence (AI) technologies are becoming increasingly instrumental in cybersecurity. By analyzing vast amounts of data, these technologies can identify anomalies and suspicious behavior that may signal a breach or an impending attack. Specifically, AI-driven analytics can significantly augment threat detection capabilities, allowing organizations to respond swiftly to threats as they arise.

For example, a major healthcare organization began utilizing an AI-based security platform to monitor its network and gain insights into user behavior. The AI system learned from historical data and established a baseline for what constituted normal activity within the organization's network. Over time, the system identified deviations from this baseline, flagging unusual behavior patterns that could indicate a potential security incident.

With the AI platform in place, the healthcare organization was able to detect and mitigate threats before they could escalate. The AI-powered alerts provided actionable insights that informed the organization's incident response strategy, ensuring that any potential breaches were addressed quickly and effectively. Additionally, the integration of AI into cybersecurity processes enhanced the organization's compliance efforts, as the real-time data monitoring allowed them to maintain accurate records for regulatory audits.

To illustrate the transformative impact of these innovations, we can delve into case studies of organizations that have successfully implemented various cybersecurity tools to improve their compliance efforts. Each of these case studies showcases not only the tools used but also the methodologies employed and the challenges faced during implementation.

A notable case study involves a global logistics company that struggled with maintaining compliance with the International Standards Organization (ISO) 27001. The organization had previously relied on a patchwork of manual processes and outdated technologies, resulting in compliance gaps and inefficiencies. To address these issues, the company implemented an integrated compliance management platform that included automated risk assessments, audit management, and policy management.

The implementation of this platform revolutionized the company's approach to compliance. By automating key processes, the organization enabled its compliance team to focus on risk mitigation rather than administrative tasks. The platform's real-time dashboards provided visibility into compliance status, serving as a crucial tool for both compliance audits and internal assessments.

The impact of the new system was profound. Not only did the logistics company achieve ISO 27001 certification, but it also reduced compliance-related incidents by 50% in the first year. The streamlined processes enhanced overall operational efficiency, and the company noted a significant improvement in employee accountability toward compliance practices.

Another inspirational example comes from a healthcare organization dealing with compliance challenges associated with the Health Insurance Portability and Accountability Act (HIPAA). Concerned about the potential risks of a data breach and the implications of HIPAA violations, the organization sought to improve its data security measures. They decided to implement a comprehensive framework that included a combination of threat intelligence platforms and advanced encryption methods.

By employing a threat intelligence platform, the organization was able to gain insights into the evolving threat landscape specific to healthcare data. The real-time alerts allowed the security team to assess vulnerabilities and adjust their defenses accordingly. Coupled with the adoption of end-to-end encryption for sensitive data, the healthcare organization significantly strengthened its compliance posture.

The results were transformative. The organization achieved compliance by ensuring data protection was not only a regulatory requirement but a core value of its operations. The combination of proactive threat awareness and robust encryption not only safeguarded sensitive patient information but also boosted the organization's reputation among stakeholders and clients.

Finally, there is the case study of a retail company that implemented AI-driven analytics to enhance its cybersecurity defenses. Facing increasing incidents of credit card fraud and data breaches, the organization recognized the need for a more sophisticated approach to tackle the growing threats. By investing in an AI security solution, the company could analyze customer transactions and identify suspicious patterns that may indicate fraud.

The implementation phase of this AI-based system involved extensive tuning of algorithms to understand the nuances of legitimate transactions versus fraudulent activities. Over a 12-month period, the organization saw a marked decline in successful fraud attempts, reinforcing customer trust and ensuring compliance with the Payment Card Industry Data Security Standard (PCI DSS).

The success of these implementations suggests that the right combination of innovative tools, driven by a forward-thinking strategy, can have a tremendously positive impact on compliance efforts across various industries. As organizations navigate the dynamic landscape of cybersecurity, they must embrace these advancements and leverage them as part of their overarching compliance strategies.

In conclusion, the current landscape of cybersecurity tools is marked by groundbreaking innovations that are fundamentally reshaping how organizations approach compliance and security. From automated compliance solutions that streamline management processes to threat intelligence platforms that enhance situational awareness and advanced encryption methods that protect sensitive data, these technologies empower companies to proactively defend against cyber threats.

By examining real-world case studies, we see that organizations implementing these innovative tools are not only better equipped to meet compliance demands but also enjoy improved operational efficiencies, strengthened reputations, and enhanced trust with stakeholders. As we look to the future, it is crucial for organizations to stay informed about emerging technologies and continuously adapt their cybersecurity strategies, ensuring that they remain resilient amidst an evolving threat landscape. Embracing innovation in cybersecurity is not merely a choice but a necessity for organizations committed to thriving in the digital world.

The Role of AI in Cyber Defense

In recent years, artificial intelligence (AI) has emerged as a powerful ally in the ongoing battle against cyber threats. As organizations increasingly rely on digital infrastructure, the complexity and volume of cyberattacks have surged. Traditional security measures often struggle to keep pace with the rapid evolution of these threats, necessitating the deployment of innovative technologies. AI has proven to be a transformative force in this realm, fundamentally reshaping the way cybersecurity efforts are conceived, executed, and managed.

AI enhances threat detection capabilities in several ways. By leveraging machine learning algorithms, AI systems can analyze vast amounts of data in real time, identifying patterns and anomalies that may indicate malicious activity. Unlike traditional security systems that rely on predefined signatures of known threats, AI can adaptively learn from new data, continuously refining its detection criteria. This capability is vital given the increasing prevalence of sophisticated attacks, such as zero-day exploits and advanced persistent threats (APTs), which often evade standard security measures.

A compelling example of AI's effectiveness in threat detection is the use of advanced anomaly detection systems. Traditional security information and event management (SIEM) tools often trigger alerts based on known threat signatures. In contrast, AI-driven platforms analyze user behavior, network traffic, and endpoint activity, establishing a baseline of "normal" operations. When deviations from this baseline occur, such as a user accessing sensitive data at unusual hours or an unexpected surge in file transfers, AI systems trigger alerts for further investigation. This proactive approach drastically reduces the time it takes to identify potential breaches, empowering organizations to respond swiftly to threats.

One notable case study illustrating the efficacy of AI in threat detection is the implementation of IBM's Watson for Cyber Security, which combines AI and machine learning to enhance the investigation of security incidents. Leveraging its natural language processing capabilities, Watson can digest and analyze unstructured data from various sources, including security alerts, threat intelligence feeds, and even academic publications. In practical terms, this has enabled security analysts to rapidly sift through vast quantities of information, uncovering insights that would have previously taken hours or even days to identify. Organizations employing Watson have reported accelerated incident response times and improved accuracy in threat assessment, showcasing AI's capacity to transform cybersecurity operations.

Beyond threat detection, AI excels in automating compliance monitoring. As regulations governing data protection and privacy continue to proliferate across industries, organizations face increasing pressure to demonstrate adherence to complex compliance frameworks, such as the General Data Protection Regulation (GDPR) and the Health Insurance Portability and Accountability Act (HIPAA). Manual compliance audits are often resource-intensive and prone to error, leaving organizations vulnerable to oversight and potential penalties.

AI-driven compliance solutions automate data monitoring and reporting, streamlining the compliance process. For instance, natural language processing algorithms can automatically analyze policy documents and data handling practices, ensuring that organizations remain aligned with legal requirements. Furthermore, AI can continuously monitor user activity, flagging any behaviors that may violate compliance policies or indicate potential data breaches. This proactive approach empowers organizations to detect and address compliance issues before they escalate into significant legal or financial repercussions.

A shining example of AI's role in compliance monitoring can be found in platforms like Protego, which leverage AI to facilitate continuous compliance assessments. Protego's software automatically scans internal policies, data access permissions, and user activities, comparing them against regulatory standards. For example, if an employee accesses personally identifiable information (PII) without the required authorization, the system generates an alert for compliance officers. The integration of AI into these processes not only reduces the burden on compliance teams but also enhances the overall security posture of the organization.

The rapid response capabilities of AI are another critical advantage in the field of cyber defense. In the event of a detected threat, organizations must be equipped to respond swiftly to minimize potential damage. AI enhances response times by automating many incident response processes. This automation allows security teams to focus on strategic decision-making, rather than getting bogged down in repetitive tasks.

Consider a scenario in which a ransomware attack is initiated against an organization. In a traditional setup, security analysts may spend significant time manually analyzing logs and attempting to identify the source of the attack. However, an AI-driven incident response platform can automatically contain the threat by isolating affected systems, deploying patches, and even blocking malicious IP addresses in real-time. By minimizing human intervention during the initial response phase, organizations can significantly reduce the potential impact of a cyberattack.

One such solution is the use of AI-driven Security Orchestration, Automation, and Response (SOAR) platforms. These platforms integrate with an organization's security tools and automate incident response workflows based on predefined playbooks. For example, if a phishing email is detected, the AI system can automatically remove it from all inboxes, inform the affected employees, and launch a security awareness campaign to prevent future incidents. This level of automation not only enhances the speed and efficiency of incident response but also helps organizations maintain a proactive stance against evolving threats.

As organizations begin to embrace AI technologies, it is crucial to examine the ethical considerations that come with their deployment in cybersecurity. One of the foremost concerns revolves around the balance between automation and human oversight. While AI systems can process vast amounts of data and respond to incidents with remarkable speed, they are not infallible. Relying solely on automated solutions without human intervention can lead to unintended consequences, such as false positives or the overlooking of nuanced attacks that require human intuition to identify.

For instance, an AI system may flag a legitimate login attempt by an employee as a potential threat due to unusual activity patterns. If human analysts are not involved in the final decision-making process, this could lead to unnecessary alarms, wasted resources, and disruptions to normal business operations. Therefore, organizations must adopt a hybrid approach that leverages AI's strengths while maintaining a critical human element in the cybersecurity strategy. This includes fostering a culture of collaboration between human analysts and AI systems, ensuring that human expertise complements automated threat detection and response capabilities.

Furthermore, ethical considerations extend to data privacy and bias in AI-driven solutions. The algorithms powering AI systems are often trained on historical data, which can inadvertently introduce biases that affect their effectiveness. If the training data reflects systemic biases, the AI system may misinterpret legitimate behavior as malicious, particularly in cases involving marginalized groups.

Organizations must recognize and address these biases during the development and implementation of AI-driven tools. Robust measures should be put in place to audit the algorithms continually and ensure that they maintain fairness and accuracy across diverse contexts.

As the field of cybersecurity continues to evolve, it is essential for organizations to stay informed about the rapid advancements in AI technologies. In doing so, they can harness the full potential of these innovations to strengthen their security posture. However, organizations must also remain vigilant regarding the ethical considerations associated with AI adoption. By fostering an adaptable and ethical AI culture, organizations can not only enhance their cybersecurity capabilities but also contribute to a more equitable and responsible technological landscape.

In summary, artificial intelligence has emerged as a transformative force in cybersecurity, enhancing threat detection, automating compliance monitoring, and improving response times. AI-driven security solutions enable organizations to stay one step ahead of ever-evolving cyber threats, increasing efficiency while mitigating risks. Real-world examples illustrate the effectiveness of AI applications in threat detection, compliance monitoring, and incident response, showcasing the tangible benefits they provide. However, as organizations embrace AI technologies, ethical considerations must be at the forefront of their approach. By balancing automation with human oversight and addressing bias and data privacy concerns, organizations can leverage AI to create a more secure and equitable digital landscape. Ultimately, AI represents a powerful tool in the ongoing quest to safeguard sensitive data and protect the integrity of our digital realm.

Future Innovations on the Horizon

The cybersecurity landscape is experiencing a rapid transformation, influenced by technological advancements that are reshaping the way organizations protect their digital assets. As we peer into the horizon of future innovations, we encounter a wealth of emerging technologies poised to redefine cybersecurity practices, enhance compliance mechanisms, and fuel the evolution of a more secure digital environment. This exploration of future innovations illuminates not only the trends and predictions emerging from experts in the field but also the proactive approach organizations must adopt to effectively integrate these developments into their cybersecurity strategies.

One of the most significant trends on the horizon is the ongoing evolution of artificial intelligence (AI) and machine learning (ML) technologies. As these innovations become more sophisticated, they hold the potential to dramatically enhance threat detection and response capabilities. AI-driven systems are already being harnessed to analyze vast amounts of data in real time, identifying patterns and anomalies that would be impossible for human analysts to discern. Future iterations of these systems are expected to harness even more advanced algorithms, enabling predictive analytics that can anticipate cyber threats before they materialize.

According to industry experts, the AI revolution in cybersecurity will likely manifest in several key areas. First, intelligent threat detection systems will evolve to incorporate adaptive learning capabilities, allowing them to refine their models based on evolving attack vectors and tactics employed by cybercriminals. This means organizations will be equipped with tools that not only respond to known threats but are also capable of dynamically adjusting to newly identified risks. The challenge, however, lies in ensuring these AI systems themselves are not vulnerable to adversarial attacks that could manipulate their outputs.

In tandem with AI advancements, the rise of automation in cybersecurity processes is set to enhance compliance efforts. Automated compliance solutions can streamline the burden of regulatory adherence, particularly in complex environments where organizations juggle multiple frameworks and standards. These tools consolidate compliance data, facilitate audits, and generate reports with minimal manual intervention, reducing the potential for human error. As organizations seek efficiency gains amidst increasing regulatory pressures, automation will be a crucial enabler in maintaining compliance while freeing up resources for more strategic initiatives.

Furthermore, the expansion of cloud computing and the incorporation of edge computing technologies present both opportunities and challenges in the compliance landscape. As organizations increasingly migrate operations to the cloud, the demand for robust security measures that preserve data integrity and privacy will intensify. Innovations in cloud security will be pivotal, with developments such as confidential computing emerging to safeguard sensitive data even in environments that are inherently shared or multi-tenant.

Emerging technologies, such as distributed ledger technology (DLT) and blockchain, are also set to play a transformative role in cybersecurity. DLT ensures transparency and immutability, making it an appealing solution for secure transactions and data integrity. In the context of compliance, these technologies can enhance audit trails, enabling organizations to provide verifiable proof of compliance with regulatory requirements. However, organizations must also grapple with the complexities of integrating blockchain solutions into existing cybersecurity frameworks, ensuring they address scalability, interoperability, and regulatory nuances.

The convergence of Internet of Things (IoT) devices and cybersecurity represents another fertile ground for future innovations. As IoT adoption proliferates, the security implications of connecting an ever-growing array of devices become more pronounced. Future innovations are expected to focus on embedding advanced security features directly into IoT devices, shifting toward a 'security by design' approach. These features might include capabilities to perform secure software updates, decentralized identity management, and end-to-end encryption for data in transit and at rest.

As organizations embrace these advances, they must do so with an eye toward maintaining compliance. Compliance frameworks will need to adapt to account for the unique vulnerabilities and risks posed by an increasing reliance on IoT technologies. For example, regulations may evolve to incorporate specific cybersecurity standards for IoT devices, ensuring that manufacturers and organizations alike prioritize security in the lifecycle of these products.

In addition to technical advancements, the importance of human factors in cybersecurity cannot be overlooked. As the technological landscape shifts, so too must the skills and capabilities of cybersecurity professionals. Future training initiatives will need to emphasize hybrid skills that blend technical acumen with a strong understanding of compliance requirements. Upskilling and reskilling the workforce to respond to technological changes will not only enhance organizational resilience but also cultivate a culture of cybersecurity awareness and accountability.

Industry experts predict that interdisciplinary collaboration will become increasingly vital as organizations navigate the complexities of compliance in the face of technological innovation. Security, legal, and compliance teams will need to work in unison to develop holistic strategies that align with both technological advancements and regulatory requirements. This collaborative ethos will drive the development of more comprehensive security frameworks, ultimately fostering a more proactive approach to compliance.

Moreover, the landscape of cyber insurance is poised for transformation in light of future innovations. As organizations implement advanced technologies and embrace automation, insurers will need to develop tailored policies that reflect the evolving risk profiles of their clients. Future innovations in cybersecurity will result in a more data-driven approach to underwriting, where insurers leverage real-time security posture data to assess risk accurately. This shift will encourage organizations to prioritize robust security measures and compliance initiatives, as their insurance premiums will be directly tied to their cybersecurity practices.

As we look ahead, the emergence of quantum computing presents both promise and peril for cybersecurity. While quantum computing has the potential to revolutionize processing capabilities, it also poses formidable challenges to encryption standards as we know them. Organizations will need to remain vigilant about the implications of quantum threats and explore the integration of quantum-resistant encryption algorithms into their compliance strategies. Proactive measures in this realm will enable organizations to stay ahead of a potential quantum revolution, ensuring that they maintain the confidentiality and integrity of sensitive data.

The impact of global events and geopolitical factors cannot be overlooked either. Cybersecurity compliance will increasingly be influenced by international collaboration and conflict. As organizations operate on a global scale, they must navigate varying regulatory frameworks that reflect differing attitudes toward privacy, security, and data ownership. Embracing international standards and aligning with best practices will be essential for organizations seeking to navigate the regulatory landscape effectively and avoid potential penalties.

As these innovations unfold, organizations must adopt a mindset of continuous learning and adaptation. Keeping abreast of emerging trends and technologies will be critical in anticipating changes within the cybersecurity landscape. Organizations can leverage thought leadership, conferences, and industry research to stay informed about upcoming innovations and their implications for compliance. Additionally, fostering a culture of agility will empower teams to respond swiftly to evolving threats and embrace new technologies that augment their security efforts.

In conclusion, the future of cybersecurity compliance will undoubtedly be shaped by a myriad of innovations on the horizon. The interplay of artificial intelligence, automation, cloud technologies, blockchain, IoT, and quantum computing presents both opportunities and challenges that organizations must be prepared to navigate. By remaining vigilant, adaptable, and proactive, organizations can leverage these advancements to not only stay ahead of compliance challenges but also build a more resilient digital landscape. As we embark on this journey of exploration and innovation, the guardians of the digital realm will find themselves equipped with the tools and insights needed to thrive in an ever-evolving cybersecurity landscape.

Chapter 9: Non-Compliance Nightmares: What to Avoid

Common Pitfalls in Cybersecurity Compliance

In the fast-evolving world of cybersecurity, compliance is a crucial cornerstone for any organization looking to safeguard sensitive data and maintain operational integrity. However, the path to regulatory adherence can be fraught with obstacles. This subchapter explores the most common pitfalls organizations face in their cybersecurity compliance efforts, drawn from both industry case studies and firsthand experiences. By highlighting these mistakes and offering practical solutions, we aim to arm readers with the knowledge necessary to navigate the compliance landscape effectively.

One of the most significant pitfalls organizations encounter is the lack of comprehensive documentation. Documentation is not just a bureaucratic hurdle; it serves as the bedrock of compliance and governance. Without accurate records of policies, procedures, and the rationale behind them, organizations risk falling into the trap of ambiguity. This can lead to inconsistent practices and unexpected regulatory scrutiny.

Take, for instance, the case of a mid-sized financial institution that invested heavily in cybersecurity tools but neglected to document its operational procedures. When a cybersecurity incident occurred, resulting in unauthorized access to customer accounts, the lack of documentation worked against them during the investigation. With no clear records outlining how security measures were intended to operate, the auditors found numerous gaps in compliance, leading to hefty fines and a tarnished reputation.

Moreover, negligence in documentation can lead to misunderstandings within teams. Employees might engage with policies that they don't fully comprehend, resulting in actions that inadvertently breach compliance mandates. For example, a tech start-up implemented a data encryption policy but failed to provide thorough documentation and training on it. When auditors came in, they discovered that employees were not encrypting data as required, leading to severe penalties.

To avoid falling into the documentation trap, organizations should prioritize the creation and maintenance of compliance-related documents. Regular updates are essential, particularly when regulations change or new technologies are adopted. Furthermore, all employees should have access to these documents, tailored in a way that is easy to understand. Establishing a documentation culture can mean hosting training sessions that both educate and empower staff to engage with the materials.

Closely related to documentation is the failure to conduct regular audits. Many organizations mistakenly assume that achieving compliance is a one-time effort. The reality is that regulatory frameworks are frequently updated to address new threats; therefore, what was once compliant may no longer meet the requirements.

Consider the example of a healthcare organization that complied with HIPAA regulations in 2017. Initially, they adopted all necessary compliance measures and even received recognition for their robust security practices. However, a lack of regular auditing left them unaware of changes to HIPAA provisions in 2019 concerning data sharing practices. When a security breach occurred and patient records were exposed due to a lapse in compliance, the organization faced not only legal penalties but also a loss of patient trust.

Regular audits should not be confined to an annual review but should be integrated as an ongoing process. Organizations should set up a compliance calendar that outlines when audits will take place, how they will be conducted, and who will take responsibility for them. Additionally, bringing in third-party auditors can provide an independent viewpoint that helps to uncover vulnerabilities that internal teams might overlook. Vulnerability assessments, penetration testing, and compliance checks can help maintain a robust security posture.

Another prominent pitfall is underestimating the importance of ongoing training and awareness programs. Compliance is dynamic; regulations evolve, and employees need to understand not just what policies exist but why they matter. A typical oversight occurs when organizations provide initial training upon hiring but neglect to implement ongoing education. This can lead employees to forget critical compliance requirements over time.

A stark example lies in a multinational corporation in the retail sector that faced regulatory action due to repeated data leaks. Their initial onboarding program introduced employees to data security protocols, but they did not reinforce this knowledge through repeated training or updates. When a data breach occurred, investigators found that key employees were unable to recall essential protocols, illustrating how compliance fatigue can set in without consistent engagement from organizations.

To fortify compliance efforts, organizations should institute continuous training that adjusts according to the latest threats and regulations. Utilizing e-learning platforms can facilitate this ongoing education, enabling employees to engage with the latest security protocols at their own pace. Regular refreshers and scenario-based training can keep compliance top of mind and help embed a culture of security awareness.

A fourth common pitfall is the failure to involve all stakeholders in the compliance journey. Many organizations approach cybersecurity compliance as an IT department issue, sidelining other critical areas such as human resources, legal, and operations. This siloed approach can create blind spots in the organization's compliance posture, leading to ineffective measures that do not account for holistic risks.

For example, if a marketing department launches a campaign that relies on customer data without adequate consultation with the compliance team, they may inadvertently violate data protection laws. In one notable case, a large tech company faced substantial fines when its marketing practices clashed with GDPR regulations, leading to public backlash and significant reputation damage.

To overcome this barrier, organizations should foster a culture of collaboration among all departments. Establishing a compliance committee that includes representatives from IT, HR, legal, and operational teams can create a unified approach to addressing compliance matters. Regular interdepartmental meetings can ensure that compliance challenges are addressed collectively, making it easier to identify vulnerabilities that may span multiple areas of the organization.

Another major oversight involves neglecting to assess third-party risks. Many organizations rely on a host of vendors and partners for operational functions, each introducing unique compliance challenges. The data breaches caused by third-party vendors are becoming alarmingly common, showing that organizations cannot overlook their supply chain's compliance status.

Take, for instance, a health services company that outsourced patient management to a third-party vendor. While the organization adhered to HIPAA regulations, its vendor had outdated security measures that led to a large data breach, compromising thousands of patient records. The health services company faced penalties for its vendor's lack of compliance, illustrating that negligence in third-party risk assessments can have devastating outcomes.

Organizations must implement thorough due diligence when onboarding third-party partners, requiring them to demonstrate compliance with relevant regulations and laws. Vendor risk assessments can include regular audits and security checks to ensure that partners maintain their compliance posture. Mutual accountability can be reinforced through contracts that stipulate compliance standards and responsibilities.

Organizations also frequently underestimate the importance of incident response planning. When breaches occur, having a proactive response strategy is vital to mitigating damage and satisfying regulatory obligations. A lack of preparation can lead to haphazard and delayed responses, which can exacerbate the situation.

An example can be seen in a prominent e-commerce company that suffered a significant data breach, exposing credit card information of millions of customers. Lacking an effective incident response plan, the organization struggled to manage communication with stakeholders. Regulatory authorities levied heavy fines due to the company's inability to notify customers in a timely manner, resulting in financial losses and reputational damage.

To prevent such scenarios, organizations must develop and maintain a robust incident response plan that details specific actionable steps to take in the event of a cyber incident. Conducting regular tabletop exercises can test the plan's effectiveness and identify areas where improvements are needed. Reinforcing the importance of timely communication can help minimize repercussions and maintain trust with customers.

Lastly, organizations often ignore the technological aspect of compliance, failing to keep their cybersecurity tools and systems updated. Compliance requirements, especially those relating to data protection and privacy, demand that organizations deploy current technologies to protect sensitive information effectively. Neglecting to upgrade systems leaves organizations vulnerable to emerging threats.

In another instance, a financial services firm faced severe penalties for its outdated software, which was not compliant with the new PCI DSS requirements. They attempted to maintain compliance with obsolete technology, which had multiple vulnerabilities that were exploited by cybercriminals. The firm not only faced fines but also lost client trust, resulting in a significant drop in revenue.

To avoid falling into this continual upgrade pitfall, organizations must routinely assess their technology stack against regulatory standards and industry best practices. Implementing a technology refresh cycle can provide a structured approach for system upgrades and replacements, ensuring that all tools remain effective and compliant.

In summary, organizations need to be acutely aware of the pitfalls that can derail their cybersecurity compliance efforts. This subchapter has outlined some of the most common mistakes, including inadequate documentation, a lack of regular audits, insufficient ongoing training, and the failure to engage all stakeholders. It is crucial for organizations to broaden their scope and assess third-party risks, maintain a proactive incident response plan, and keep their technology updated.

By carefully examining these pitfalls and recognizing their potential impact, organizations can take action to strengthen their compliance frameworks. Compliance should not be a mere checkbox or a series of distant tasks; it must be an integrated aspect of the organizational culture where leaders and employees work collaboratively towards shared cybersecurity objectives. Empowering individuals within the organization with knowledge and resources is not just beneficial—it's essential. The journey toward compliance is ongoing, and continuous vigilance will remain key to navigating the complex world of cybersecurity while ensuring that organizations can thrive in a landscape fraught with obstacles.

The Cost of Non-Compliance

Non-compliance in the realm of cybersecurity is not just a theoretical concern; it comes with tangible costs that can cripple organizations financially and irreparably damage their reputations. The seriousness of this issue gained heightened visibility in recent years, with the proliferation of data breaches and the rising scrutiny from regulators. Each incident serves as a stark reminder of the realities organizations face when they fail to meet compliance requirements.

The financial implications of non-compliance can be staggering. According to a report from the Ponemon Institute, the average total cost of a data breach in 2023 was estimated at $4.24 million. This figure represents an increase of more than 10% compared to previous years, a trend that underscores the escalating consequences for organizations that do not prioritize cybersecurity compliance. These costs arise from various factors, including forensic investigations, incident response, notification of affected individuals, legal fees, regulatory penalties, and potential loss of business due to decreased consumer trust.

Consider the case of Target Corporation, which faced a massive data breach in late 2013. The breach compromised the credit card information of nearly 40 million customers and the personal information of an additional 70 million individuals. Target's non-compliance with basic security protocols resulted in a staggering financial fallout, amounting to over $162 million in expenses related to the breach. Additionally, the company faced a settlement of $18.5 million in a multistate lawsuit. The reputational damage was no less severe, as public trust wavered and the customer base shifted to competitors. The chilling effect of such incidents highlights the undeniable truth: the costs of non-compliance can extend far beyond initial financial penalties.

In interviews with industry experts, the long-term impacts of non-compliance become even clearer. Sarah Thompson, a cybersecurity consultant with over a decade of experience, articulates that the effects of a single breach can ripple through an organization for years. “The immediate costs of dealing with a breach are only part of the equation,” she explains. “Organizations often underestimate the lasting damage to their reputation and customer loyalty. The road to recovery is long and arduous, and businesses must proactively demonstrate their commitment to security to regain trust.”

The reputational toll of a data breach can manifest in various ways. Companies that have suffered breaches often experience a drop in stock prices, increased scrutiny from investors, and heightened skepticism from customers. A study by the University of California, Berkeley, found that publicly traded companies suffer an average stock price decline of 5% in the days following a breach announcement. For large corporations like Equifax, the fallout was even more severe; the company saw its stock value diminish by nearly 30% after disclosing a breach affecting 147 million consumers. The loss of consumer trust can lead to curtailed revenue streams and challenges in acquiring new customers, amplifying the long-term financial impacts tied to non-compliance.

Moreover, the regulatory landscape surrounding data protection is evolving rapidly, with authorities imposing stricter compliance requirements. Regulations such as the General Data Protection Regulation (GDPR) in Europe and the California Consumer Privacy Act (CCPA) have introduced hefty penalties for non-compliance. For instance, GDPR violations can result in fines of up to 20 million euros or 4% of the company's annual global revenue, whichever is higher. This means that the financial stakes for organizations that fail to adhere to compliance standards are higher than ever before.

David Ramirez, a legal expert specializing in cybersecurity regulations, emphasizes the urgency for organizations to prioritize compliance: "Failure to comply with regulations not only invites punitive measures but can also lead to class-action lawsuits from consumers whose data has been compromised. The legal landscape is evolving, and organizations must be responsive to this reality."

One particularly illustrative case involved Facebook's run-ins with regulatory authorities. In July 2019, the Federal Trade Commission (FTC) fined Facebook $5 billion for privacy violations related to the Cambridge Analytica scandal. This case exemplifies how non-compliance with data protection regulations can lead to monumental fines, not to mention the public relations nightmare Facebook endured as its practices became the subject of intense scrutiny. Beyond the immediate financial penalty, the company's reputation took a significant hit, with trust levels plummeting among users and advertisers alike.

In the wake of high-profile breaches, organizations have also confronted increased scrutiny from customers and stakeholders. Many consumers are becoming more discerning, actively choosing to engage with businesses that demonstrate a commitment to protecting their data. A survey conducted by IBM Security revealed that approximately 78% of consumers believe organizations must be responsible for protecting their data. When companies fail to meet these expectations, they risk losing business to competitors that prioritize compliance and data protection.

Moreover, the operational impacts of non-compliance cannot be overstated. Businesses that experience a breach may find themselves embroiled in lengthy and costly recovery efforts. For example, a significant breach necessitates an extensive forensic investigation, often leading to the involvement of external cybersecurity firms. These investigations can take weeks or months, diverting valuable resources away from core business operations. This disruption can stifle productivity and hinder innovation, as organizations are forced to allocate budgets and manpower that would otherwise be used to further development initiatives.

In interviews with professionals involved in cybersecurity incident response, some experts shared anecdotes about organizations facing dire situations due to non-compliance. For instance, one IT manager recounted a situation in which a hospital's patient records were compromised due to inadequate security measures. The organization underwent a devastating investigation, leading to operational disruptions that impacted patient care delivery. “The breach impacted our ability to serve patients effectively,” he states. “We were in crisis mode, focusing all our attention on remediation, rather than providing essential services.”

The cybersecurity landscape continues to evolve, with attackers finding innovative ways to exploit security vulnerabilities. Consequently, organizations that ignore compliance run the risk of becoming prime targets for cybercriminals. As the sophistication of cyber threats grows, so too does the likelihood of organizations experiencing costly breaches. A startling report from Cybersecurity Ventures predicts that the cost of cybercrime globally will reach $10.5 trillion annually by 2025. Failure to invest in compliance frameworks that mitigate these risks can lead to devastating financial fallout.

Furthermore, organizations that neglect compliance may encounter an array of indirect costs. Loss of intellectual property, reputational consequences, and diminished employee morale can all stem from non-compliance incidents. For example, a manufacturing company that suffered a data breach lost proprietary information related to product designs, resulting in an inability to maintain a competitive edge. The company's inability to innovate meant it surrendered market share to competitors, leading to further financial repercussions that could have been mitigated through adherence to compliance standards.

In understanding the true costs of non-compliance, organizations must also recognize the cumulative effect of regulatory penalties that can arise in response to a breach. In addition to facing fines, organizations may also be subject to increased scrutiny in future audits and assessments. Once a company has been flagged for non-compliance, regulators are likely to keep a closer watch on their operations, leading to potential prolonged consequences that can hinder growth.

Take, for instance, the case of Yahoo, which suffered a massive data breach in 2013 affecting all three billion users. Despite the large settlement figure of $85 million that Yahoo agreed to, the long-term impact on its credibility was far more detrimental, especially as it navigated the sale to Verizon. The acquisition was ultimately reduced by $350 million as Verizon sought to reduce liability over the fallout of the breach. Such instances illustrate how regulatory penalties can lead to arduous negotiations and settlements that stretch for years after an incident.

In light of these repercussions, organizations must approach compliance not merely as a checklist they must complete but as an ongoing process that is critical to their survival in today's digital landscape. Moving forward, it is essential for businesses to integrate compliance initiatives into their core strategy, ensuring alignment among key stakeholders in order to build a culture of cybersecurity awareness. This involves creating comprehensive training programs that empower employees to understand their roles in maintaining security and adherence to regulations.

By taking proactive measures, organizations can mitigate the risk of non-compliance and its associated costs. Implementing continuous monitoring programs, regular security audits, and risk assessments can provide organizations with insight into their current security posture, enabling them to identify vulnerabilities before they can be exploited. As Richard Green, a cybersecurity adviser, remarks, "Maintaining compliance requires full organizational commitment. It's a shared responsibility that extends beyond IT departments."

The evolution of cybersecurity compliance necessitates that organizations remain agile and responsive to new regulations, emerging threats, and best practices to protect their digital assets. Organizations that successfully navigate the compliance landscape will not only avoid the costs associated with non-compliance but will also strengthen their reputation and build lasting trust with customers.

Investing in compliance is not just about avoiding penalties; it creates opportunities for businesses to distinguish themselves in a crowded marketplace. Organizations with a strong commitment to data protection can promote themselves as trustworthy leaders in their respective industries, gaining a competitive edge in the eyes of consumers who prioritize security.

As we conclude this subchapter, it's essential to underscore the overarching lesson: the costs of non-compliance are extensive and multifaceted. From financial penalties to reputational damage and operational disruptions, the consequences can devastate an organization, stretching far beyond the initial breaches. Understanding these costs provides a powerful incentive for businesses to prioritize compliance.

In an era where data breaches are an unfortunate reality, organizations must proactively adapt their compliance strategies to protect themselves and their stakeholders. By investing in robust cybersecurity frameworks and fostering a culture of compliance, organizations can emerge as the guardians of the digital realm, safeguarding their assets and the trust of their customers. The journey ahead may be fraught with challenges, but the commitment to compliance will ultimately yield significant dividends in ensuring long-term success in the ever-evolving landscape of cybersecurity.

Turning Non-Compliance into Opportunity

In the world of cybersecurity compliance, the stakes are high, and the threats are ever-evolving. While organizations often focus on avoiding non-compliance nightmares, there exists an alternative perspective that can transform these potential disasters into powerful opportunities for growth and improvement. By embracing the lessons learned from non-compliance incidents, businesses can enhance their security posture, foster innovation, and strengthen their overall resilience in the face of cyber threats.

The journey of compliance is not merely a checkbox exercise but rather an ongoing process that requires constant evaluation, adaptation, and improvement. This chapter aims to illuminate how organizations can turn their compliance challenges into stepping stones for success, encouraging a proactive mindset that sees compliance as a critical component of their operational strategy.

To illustrate this transformative approach, we will examine several case studies of organizations that have confronted compliance failures head-on, emerging stronger and more versatile in their cybersecurity practices as a result. Each of these examples serves as a testament to the idea that setbacks can lead to significant advancements when approached with a growth-oriented mindset.

One such exemplary case involves a medium-sized healthcare provider that experienced a data breach due to inadequate protection of sensitive patient information. The incident exposed the organization to severe regulatory penalties under HIPAA, resulting in hefty fines and significant reputational damage. Initially grappling with the fallout from the breach, the organization faced staunch criticism from stakeholders and patients alike. However, instead of adopting a defensive posture, the leadership team recognized this as an opportunity for substantial improvement.

In the wake of the breach, the organization initiated a comprehensive audit of its existing cybersecurity practices. It brought in an outside consulting firm specializing in cybersecurity compliance to assess vulnerabilities and areas of weakness. These experts conducted thorough risk assessments, identifying gaps in the organization's ability to protect patient data effectively. Armed with this information, the organization prioritized its security upgrades, investing in advanced encryption technologies and robust access controls.

Moreover, the organization adopted a culture of continuous improvement by implementing regular training programs for employees. This comprehensive education initiative emphasized data protection and cybersecurity awareness, ensuring that all staff members understood their respective roles in safeguarding sensitive information. By fostering a security-first approach across all levels of operation, the organization turned an unfortunate breach into an opportunity to enhance its culture and resilience.

As a result of these initiatives, the healthcare provider not only rectified its compliance failures but also cultivated a greater sense of trust among patients and stakeholders. Feedback from patients' post-breach revealed that many appreciated the transparency demonstrated by the organization throughout the recovery process. The commitment to change led to improved patient satisfaction, ultimately resulting in increased patient retention rates and enhanced brand loyalty.

Another case worth examining is that of a prominent retailer that faced a massive data breach exposing millions of customers' credit card information. The fallout resulted in legal actions, regulatory scrutiny, and millions in losses. Initially overwhelmed by the scale of the breach, the retailer's leadership decided to pivot its focus to recovery as an opportunity for acceleration rather than stagnation.

Following the breach, the company established a dedicated task force to confront its compliance challenges head-on. This task force's primary goal was to restore customer confidence while ensuring compliance with PCI DSS requirements to prevent future incidents. The retailer invested in state-of-the-art cybersecurity technologies, focused on implementing artificial intelligence-driven monitoring tools to detect anomalies in real-time. This proactive approach not only helped safeguard customer data but also reduced the time taken to identify and respond to potential threats.

Furthermore, the retailer transformed its incident response strategy into a key learning module. Each security incident would conclude with a detailed debrief, wherein team members analyzed what went wrong, what preventive measures could be taken, and how future incidents could be better handled. This distance between a breach and compliance failure gradually faded, creating a resilient cycle of learning that improved the incident response approach over time.

The outcome was nothing short of remarkable. After successfully navigating regulatory inquiries and minimizing financial losses through compliance investments, the retailer experienced a noticeable increase in online purchases within a year of the breach. Customers cited improved security measures and better digital experiences as significant factors influencing their return to the brand. By revisiting its cybersecurity strategy through a lens of opportunity, the retailer solidified its market position and renewed customer loyalty.

An additional example comes from the technology sector, where a leading software company fell victim to a cyberattack that exploited vulnerabilities in its aging infrastructure. The attack not only led to the unauthorized access of customer data but also triggered a regulatory investigation due to non-compliance with GDPR's stringent data protection requirements. The consequences posed significant challenges and risks to the software company's operations and reputation.

Instead of allowing the situation to dictate their direction, the company's leadership viewed this experience as an unprecedented opportunity. They recognized the importance of rebuilding trust with customers and stakeholders, prompting them to commit to a complete overhaul of their data governance strategy.

The organization began by redesigning its entire data protection framework, ensuring compliance with the GDPR and other applicable regulations. By aligning their data management practices with best-in-class standards, they significantly improved their ability to protect customer information. They also embraced transparency, publishing detailed reports on data protection efforts, which showcased their commitment to regulatory compliance.

In tandem, the software company revitalized its product pipeline to include enhanced security features, making security a part of its value proposition. Customers viewed these innovations positively, often remarking how the company effectively turned a compliance failure into a unique selling point. The software company's proactive response demonstrated its dedication to improvement and helped foster a culture of security that permeated its entire product line.

This shift toward a proactive mindset when addressing compliance challenges requires organizations to cultivate a broader perspective on compliance. Key to this shift is the acknowledgment that compliance is not merely a regulatory obligation, but an essential component of building sustainable business practices. By embracing compliance as a continuous journey, organizations can shift their focus from fear and avoidance of penalties to proactive innovation and security enhancement.

One effective strategy organizations can implement involves encouraging a learning-oriented culture. Creating spaces where employees feel empowered to report compliance challenges or suggest improvements without fear of retribution fosters an environment where innovation can thrive. Encouraging open dialogue can lead to valuable insights into potential vulnerabilities before they manifest into serious non-compliance issues.

Additionally, a proactive approach entails staying informed about industry best practices and evolving laws to maintain compliance ahead of time. Attending conferences, workshops, and training sessions can equip cybersecurity professionals with the latest knowledge and tools needed to navigate a rapidly changing compliance landscape. Organizations may also consider collaborating with peers in their industry to share insights and strategies for ensuring compliance with regulations.

Another practical step involves engaging customers and stakeholders in discussions about compliance. By communicating openly about compliance initiatives, organizations can build trust and demonstrate a commitment to security, signaling that they prioritize the protection of sensitive data. This transparency can serve as a unifying factor, enabling a shared journey toward better compliance practices.

Moreover, organizations should conduct regular reviews of their compliance strategies, evaluating what has worked well and what needs improvement. Continual self-assessment ensures that compliance practices evolve to meet new challenges and enables organizations to remain agile in the face of changing regulations and cyber threats.

In the spirit of using non-compliance challenges as opportunities, it is essential for organizations to recognize that such experiences are valuable learning moments. By implementing or improving processes in response to a compliance failure, organizations can create a feedback loop that encourages ongoing evaluation, bolsters resilience, and ultimately, enhances security.

The lessons learned from transforming non-compliance into opportunity extend beyond the confines of individual organizations. The cybersecurity community at large benefits when members openly share their experiences and insights regarding compliance failures and successes. By investing in collective learning, organizations can develop a shared repository of knowledge that enhances the industry's overall compliance strategy. This culture of collaboration can lead to innovation and resilience at a systemic level, key attributes to combat the ever-evolving landscape of cyber threats.

In conclusion, while non-compliance poses significant risks and challenges for organizations, it can also serve as an impetus for meaningful transformation. By adopting a proactive mindset and viewing compliance as a continuous journey, organizations can harness the insights gained through non-compliance experiences to drive growth, innovation, and security enhancements. Through collaborative efforts and a commitment to ongoing improvement, organizations can transform non-compliance nightmares into opportunities for resilience, ensuring that they are well-equipped to navigate the complexities of the cybersecurity landscape while simultaneously safeguarding their most valuable assets—their data, customers, and reputation.

Chapter 10: Building Your Cyber Fortress: Tools & Resources

Essential Tools for Cybersecurity Compliance

In the ever-evolving landscape of cybersecurity, the importance of having the right tools and resources at your disposal cannot be overstated. Effective cybersecurity compliance is not merely about adhering to regulations; it's about building a robust framework that can withstand the myriad challenges posed by cyber threats while protecting sensitive data and maintaining organizational integrity. This subchapter will provide a comprehensive overview of essential tools and resources that organizations can employ to achieve and sustain compliance in an increasingly complex digital environment.

First, we will explore the various categories of tools that are vital for cybersecurity compliance, including software solutions, frameworks, and templates. Each category will be examined in detail, providing readers with insights on how these tools can be leveraged to fortify their cybersecurity infrastructure. Additionally, we will provide real-world examples and case studies showcasing how organizations have successfully implemented these tools to enhance their compliance status and overall security posture.

Software Solutions

At the heart of effective cybersecurity compliance are robust software solutions designed to manage risks, monitor security, and ensure adherence to regulations. These tools span several domains, including identity and access management (IAM), security information and event management (SIEM), vulnerability management, and data loss prevention (DLP).

Identity and Access Management (IAM)

IAM solutions are essential for protecting sensitive information by ensuring that only authorized users have access to specific data and systems. By implementing IAM solutions, organizations can enforce policies that manage user identities, control access, and maintain user privileges across various systems. Popular IAM tools include Okta, Microsoft Azure Active Directory, and OneLogin.

Okta stands out with its user-friendly interface and seamless integration with a multitude of applications. It offers features such as single sign-on, multi-factor authentication, and lifecycle management, which collectively enhance security while facilitating compliance with regulations like GDPR and HIPAA.

Microsoft Azure Active Directory (Azure AD) is another prominent player in the IAM space, providing cloud-based identity management that is particularly beneficial for organizations leveraging Microsoft's suite of products. Its robust security features, including conditional access policies and identity protection, help organizations meet compliance requirements while ensuring users have a smooth experience.

OneLogin, similar to Okta and Azure AD, offers comprehensive IAM solutions with an emphasis on ease of use and deployment. Its risk-based authentication features make it especially valuable for organizations that require a stronger security posture to protect sensitive user data.

Security Information and Event Management (SIEM)

SIEM solutions are critical in monitoring, detecting, and responding to security incidents in real time. These tools aggregate and analyze data from various sources within an organization's IT infrastructure, providing insights into potential threats and vulnerabilities. Leading SIEM solutions include Splunk, IBM QRadar, and LogRhythm.

Splunk is widely regarded for its analytical capabilities, offering organizations the ability to visualize complex datasets and uncover hidden insights. Its advanced machine learning features enable automated detection of anomalies and security threats, making it an indispensable tool for compliance monitoring.

IBM QRadar provides an integrated approach to security management, enabling organizations to centralize their data and streamline compliance efforts. Its ability to correlate events from different sources ensures that security teams have a comprehensive view of the threat landscape and can respond quickly to incidents.

LogRhythm is known for its user-friendly interface and powerful analytics. The platform's proactive threat detection capabilities, combined with a focus on compliance reporting, make it a valuable resource for organizations aiming to enhance their security posture and meet regulatory standards.

Vulnerability Management

Vulnerability management tools play a crucial role in identifying, assessing, and mitigating vulnerabilities within an organization's systems. These tools can automate scanning processes, prioritize vulnerabilities based on risk, and assist in remediation efforts. Notable vulnerability management solutions include Nessus, Qualys, and Rapid7 InsightVM.

Nessus, developed by Tenable, is recognized for its comprehensive vulnerability database and scanning capabilities. Organizations can quickly identify vulnerabilities across their IT assets and receive detailed recommendations for remediation, ensuring ongoing compliance with standards like PCI DSS and NIST.

Qualys offers a cloud-based approach to vulnerability management, allowing organizations to continuously monitor their assets for vulnerabilities. Its integrated suite of security and compliance solutions makes it easier for organizations to maintain compliance across various regulatory frameworks.

Rapid7 InsightVM provides interactive dashboards and real-time visibility into vulnerabilities across an organization's infrastructure. Its risk prioritization features and automated remediation workflows streamline the vulnerability management process, improving efficiency and compliance outcomes.

Data Loss Prevention (DLP)

DLP solutions help organizations prevent unauthorized access and sharing of sensitive data. These tools monitor and control data in use, in transit, and at rest, ensuring compliance with data protection regulations. Key DLP solutions include Symantec DLP, McAfee Total Protection for DLP, and Digital Guardian.

Symantec DLP provides a comprehensive approach to data protection, offering content detection and policy enforcement mechanisms. Its robust reporting capabilities help organizations demonstrate compliance with data regulations while managing the risk of data breaches effectively.

McAfee Total Protection for DLP offers a unified solution for data protection that includes endpoint and network DLP capabilities. Its policy templates and customizable settings make it easier for organizations to adhere to regulatory requirements and safeguard sensitive information.

Digital Guardian focuses on protecting sensitive data across all endpoints and network environments. Its ability to identify and control data flows ensures that organizations can comply with regulatory mandates while preventing data loss and breaches.

Frameworks

In addition to software solutions, using established cybersecurity frameworks can provide organizations with guidelines and best practices for achieving compliance. Frameworks such as the NIST Cybersecurity Framework

(CSF), ISO/IEC 27001, and CIS Controls can serve as foundational resources for any cybersecurity compliance strategy.

NIST Cybersecurity Framework (CSF)

The NIST CSF is a widely recognized framework that provides organizations with a flexible approach to managing cybersecurity risks. It is designed to be adaptable for organizations of various sizes and sectors, making it an ideal resource for compliance with regulations like FISMA and HIPAA.

The framework consists of five core functions: Identify, Protect, Detect, Respond, and Recover. By following these functions, organizations can develop comprehensive cybersecurity programs that enhance their resilience against cyber threats while ensuring compliance with applicable regulations.

Implementing the NIST CSF involves assessing current security practices, identifying gaps, and deploying necessary controls to mitigate risks. It provides organizations with a clear roadmap for continuous improvement, making it an invaluable tool for achieving long-term compliance goals.

ISO/IEC 27001

ISO/IEC 27001 is an international standard that outlines best practices for establishing, implementing, maintaining, and continually improving an Information Security Management System (ISMS). Achieving ISO/IEC 27001 certification demonstrates an organization's commitment to protecting sensitive information and meeting compliance requirements under various regulations.

The standard specifies a risk-based approach to information security, encouraging organizations to identify and assess risks and implement appropriate controls. The certification process involves a third-party audit, which provides credibility and assurance to customers, partners, and stakeholders regarding the organization's compliance efforts.

CIS Controls

The Center for Internet Security (CIS) Controls provides a prioritized set of cybersecurity best practices aimed at improving organizational security posture. The CIS Controls are designed to be practical and actionable, making them accessible to organizations seeking to enhance their compliance status.

The controls are structured in three categories: Basic, Foundational, and Organizational Controls. They cover a range of topics, including inventory management, vulnerability management, and incident response, guiding organizations in implementing effective cybersecurity measures that align with regulatory requirements.

Templates and Resources

Utilizing templates and additional resources can streamline the compliance process and ensure that organizations have the documentation needed to demonstrate adherence to regulatory standards. Risk assessment templates, security policy templates, and compliance checklists are among the essential materials that organizations should leverage in their compliance efforts.

Risk Assessment Templates

Risk assessment templates provide organizations with a structured approach to evaluating potential threats and vulnerabilities. These templates help organizations identify assets, assess risks, and prioritize actions to mitigate vulnerabilities. By using risk assessment templates, organizations can ensure they are adequately prepared for compliance audits and demonstrate a proactive approach to risk management.

Security Policy Templates

Developing and implementing security policies is a critical component of cybersecurity compliance. Security policy templates can guide organizations in creating comprehensive policies that address key areas, such as access control, incident response, data protection, and acceptable use. Tailoring these templates to fit specific organizational needs can strengthen overall compliance efforts and minimize potential vulnerabilities.

Compliance Checklists

Compliance checklists serve as practical tools for organizations to monitor their adherence to regulatory requirements. These checklists can outline the key requirements of various regulations, ensuring organizations stay informed and on track during the compliance process. Regularly reviewing and updating compliance checklists can help organizations maintain their compliance status and address any gaps identified.

Real-World Case Studies

To further illustrate the effectiveness of these tools and resources, this section will present case studies of organizations that have successfully implemented cybersecurity compliance strategies using these tools.

Case Study 1: HealthTech Solutions

HealthTech Solutions, a mid-sized healthcare organization, faced challenges in demonstrating compliance with HIPAA regulations. After conducting a thorough assessment of their cybersecurity landscape, they implemented a combination of IAM and DLP solutions. By adopting Okta for IAM and Symantec DLP for data protection, they were able to significantly improve their security posture.

Through Okta, HealthTech Solutions automated user provisioning and de-provisioning, ensuring that only authorized personnel had access to sensitive patient data. Meanwhile, Symantec DLP allowed the organization to monitor data flows and prevent unauthorized sharing of electronic health records. As a result, HealthTech Solutions successfully achieved compliance with HIPAA and improved its overall industry reputation.

Case Study 2: Manufacturing Innovations Corp.

Manufacturing Innovations Corp., a leader in the manufacturing industry, struggled with maintaining compliance with ISO/IEC 27001. The organization decided to adopt the NIST Cybersecurity Framework as a foundational guideline for its compliance efforts. They utilized vulnerability management solutions, like Nessus, to identify and remediate weaknesses within their infrastructure.

By implementing the NIST CSF and taking a risk-based approach to information security, Manufacturing Innovations Corp. was able to achieve ISO/IEC 27001 certification within a year. The organization's commitment to cybersecurity compliance resulted in enhanced operational efficiencies and a stronger competitive advantage in the market.

Case Study 3: FinSecure Bank

FinSecure Bank was facing increasing pressure to comply with various financial regulations, including PCI DSS. To streamline their compliance efforts, the bank invested in a comprehensive SIEM solution, IBM QRadar, to enhance its monitoring and response capabilities.

As a result of implementing QRadar, FinSecure Bank gained real-time visibility into its security events and improved incident response times. The automated reporting features enabled the bank to efficiently generate compliance reports, ensuring that it met regulatory deadlines without sacrificing security. This proactive approach ultimately enhanced their overall security posture and instilled trust among customers and stakeholders.

Conclusion

In conclusion, the landscape of cybersecurity compliance is multifaceted, requiring organizations to leverage a range of tools and resources effectively. By investing in essential software solutions, adhering to recognized frameworks, and utilizing templates and additional resources, organizations can foster a proactive compliance culture that mitigates risks and enhances their overall security posture.

The case studies demonstrate that organizations across various sectors have successfully navigated cybersecurity compliance challenges by implementing effective tools and strategies. As businesses continue to grapple with evolving threats and stringent regulations, the right combination of tools and resources will empower them to become resilient guardians of the digital realm, safeguarding sensitive information while achieving their compliance objectives. By prioritizing cybersecurity compliance as an integral part of their operations, organizations can position themselves not only as leaders in their respective industries but also as trusted stewards of the digital age.

Creating a Resourceful Ecosystem

In the rapidly evolving world of cybersecurity, creating a resourceful ecosystem is essential for effective compliance and safeguarding digital assets. An organization's cybersecurity posture is not solely a function of its technology; it is deeply rooted in the collaboration between diverse stakeholders. As cyber threats continue to increase in both frequency and sophistication, building a supportive network among IT teams, legal departments, external partners, and industry peers becomes paramount. This subchapter will delve into the significance of collaboration, the benefits of knowledge sharing, and real-world examples that underscore the power of collective effort in enhancing cybersecurity compliance.

At its core, a resourceful ecosystem is about establishing a culture of collaboration where different functions within an organization work cohesively toward common goals. IT departments, compliance officers, legal teams, and business leaders must communicate openly and share responsibility for cybersecurity outcomes. The complexity of current regulations and the barrage of cyber threats necessitate a symbiotic relationship among these groups. For example, while IT teams are responsible for implementing and managing security technologies, legal departments play a vital role in ensuring that these solutions comply with applicable laws and industry standards.

The importance of collaboration begins with establishing an ongoing dialogue between stakeholders. Regular meetings, workshops, and brainstorming sessions facilitate open lines of communication, fostering an environment where ideas and concerns can be shared freely. This collaborative approach can help organizations identify gaps in their compliance frameworks, allowing them to address potential vulnerabilities before they can be exploited.

Moreover, this dialogue serves as a valuable platform for educating stakeholders about their respective roles in cybersecurity compliance. IT professionals may not always have a thorough understanding of legal requirements, while legal experts may not be well-versed in technical aspects of cybersecurity. By bridging this knowledge gap through collaborations, organizations can enhance their overall resilience against cyber threats.

Another crucial aspect of creating a resourceful ecosystem is the effective integration of external partners into the compliance framework. The concept of 'it takes a village' is particularly relevant in cybersecurity, where organizations often interact with various third-party vendors and service providers. Whether it's a cloud service provider, a cybersecurity consulting firm, or a software vendor, these external partners can bring invaluable expertise and insights that can strengthen an organization's compliance posture.

For instance, involving external partners in regular assessments can yield fresh perspectives on vulnerabilities and potential mitigations. Joint exercises such as simulated cyberattacks or tabletop exercises can serve to enhance knowledge sharing and bolster overall preparedness. By treating external partners as integral members of the compliance ecosystem, organizations can create a dynamic environment where innovative solutions to compliance challenges can be rapidly developed.

The benefits of resource sharing within this ecosystem cannot be understated. Organizations that cultivate collaborative relationships can significantly reduce costs and improve their compliance efforts. Instead of reinventing the wheel, teams can leverage existing resources, knowledge, and even tools that collaborators are willing to share. This not only accelerates the compliance journey but also reduces the chances of duplicated efforts and inefficiencies.

Sharing best practices and lessons learned is another powerful way to enhance compliance across the ecosystem. When stakeholders come together to discuss previous experiences with compliance setbacks, they unveil valuable insights that can prevent future missteps. Real-world case studies can spark discussions about what went wrong and the strategies that can help avert such issues in the future. This shared learning environment fosters a culture of continuous improvement that can lead to innovative solutions to ongoing compliance challenges.

A compelling example of successful collaboration within a resourceful ecosystem is the story of a multinational healthcare organization that faced significant cybersecurity compliance challenges due to the variety of regulations it needed to adhere to, including HIPAA, GDPR, and other local laws. The organization recognized that to navigate the complex regulatory landscape, they needed to establish a comprehensive ecosystem that included not only internal teams but also external partners such as legal advisors, regulatory consultants, and cybersecurity firms.

The company initiated regular cross-functional meetings that included representatives from IT, compliance, legal, and external partners. These discussions facilitated the identification of regulatory ambiguities and operationalized compliance requirements in a manner that aligned with business objectives. By sharing expertise and resources, the organization was able to implement a robust compliance framework that addressed the myriad of regulations it faced, ultimately reducing risks and improving patient privacy.

Additionally, the implementation of a shared platform for documenting compliance efforts and incidents became a game-changer. This digital space allowed all stakeholders to contribute insights, share relevant resources such as templates and checklists, and maintain up-to-date logs of compliance activities. This collaborative documentation tool fostered transparency, ensuring that all parties involved were informed and accountable for their contributions to compliance efforts.

Another noteworthy example comes from the financial services sector, where a consortium of banks and financial institutions recognized the need for collective action against cyber threats. As singular entities faced challenges in keeping pace with rapidly evolving cybersecurity risks, they formed a collaborative alliance focused on knowledge sharing and resource pooling. This resource-sharing ecosystem enabled them to develop industry-wide standards for cybersecurity practices and compliance frameworks.

Through shared threat intelligence reports, coalition members can identify emerging threats and refine their cybersecurity measures collectively. The proactive sharing of incident response strategies allowed members to address vulnerabilities more efficiently and implement best practices faster than they could have done individually. As a result, the participating organizations not only strengthened their own defenses but also contributed to an overall increase in the cyber resilience of the financial services industry.

The story of this consortium demonstrates the potential for organizations to amplify one another's efforts through collaboration, enhancing compliance outcomes while simultaneously fortifying defenses against cyber threats. When entities unite for a common cause, they can achieve much more than they could in isolation.

Furthermore, fostering a resourceful ecosystem requires investing in ongoing training and awareness initiatives. Continuous education across all stakeholder groups is essential for reducing knowledge gaps and promoting a safety-first mindset within the organization. Training sessions should not only cover best practices in cybersecurity but also educate all employees about the compliance landscape, helping them to understand the significance of their roles in safeguarding sensitive data.

For instance, creating opportunities for employees from different departments to engage in joint training programs can break down silos and generate a sense of shared responsibility. Training might include scenarios highlighting how IT challenges and legal requirements intersect, demonstrating the necessity for collaboration. A comprehensive training program will ensure that every member of an organization is equipped to contribute actively to its cybersecurity compliance efforts.

Additionally, organizations should consider seeking alliances with academic institutions and research organizations. By collaborating with thought leaders in the field of cybersecurity, businesses can tap into cutting-edge research and gain insights into emerging trends. These partnerships can also yield mutually beneficial outcomes, such as internships, workshops, and knowledge exchange programs that enhance the skill sets of both teams and students.

To foster a thriving ecosystem, organizations can implement a feedback loop to assess the effectiveness of their collaborative efforts. Establishing metrics to evaluate the outcomes of partnerships and resource-sharing initiatives is critical to understanding their value. Metrics could include reduced incident response times, decreased compliance breaches, or enhanced employee awareness scores, among others. Regular assessments inform decision-making regarding future collaborations and allow for continuous improvement of the ecosystem.

One emerging practice within resourceful ecosystems is the establishment of "cyber councils" or task forces that bring together professionals from diverse backgrounds to collaborate on specific cybersecurity compliance initiatives. These councils can be composed of representatives from various departments, industry peers, and even external experts. By focusing on defined objectives, these cross-functional teams can mobilize quickly to address urgent compliance challenges, share knowledge, and drive outcomes effectively.

The creation of these councils not only enables targeted addressing of compliance issues but also cultivates a sense of community among participants. Individuals feel empowered by being part of a larger initiative, sparking enthusiasm and encouraging engagement in compliance efforts that would otherwise seem daunting in isolation.

In summary, cultivating a resourceful ecosystem for cybersecurity compliance is a multifaceted endeavor that demands intentional collaboration, resource sharing, and ongoing education. By fostering strong communication channels among stakeholders, organizations can create a collaborative environment that enhances their overall security posture. Real-world success stories demonstrate how partnerships, both internal and external, can lead to improved compliance outcomes and greater resilience against cyber threats.

To thrive in the complex landscape of cybersecurity compliance, organizations must seek out and embrace collaborations that foster shared learning and growth. From IT and legal teams to external partners and industry consortia, every stakeholder plays a critical role in fortifying the cybersecurity ecosystem. By leveraging collective expertise and insights, organizations can navigate compliance challenges with greater agility and efficiency, ultimately safeguarding sensitive data while remaining compliant in an ever-evolving regulatory landscape.

In an era marked by digital interconnectedness, the strength of any organization's cybersecurity measures will depend heavily on its ability to collaborate effectively within its ecosystem. As cyber threats continue to pose significant risks, the imperative to build robust networks of support and knowledge sharing will only grow stronger. Organizations that prioritize and invest in these collaborative relationships will be best positioned to rise to the challenges presented by the digital age, ensuring not only compliance but also the security of their digital assets and the trust of their customers.

Staying Informed: Continuous Learning and Adaptation

In the rapidly evolving realm of cybersecurity, the importance of staying informed cannot be overstated. As cyber threats become increasingly sophisticated, it is crucial for organizations and professionals to commit to continuous education and awareness. A well-informed workforce not only enhances an organization's security posture but also bolsters its compliance efforts. The landscape of cybersecurity is marked by constant change, with new technologies, regulations, and threat vectors emerging at an unprecedented pace. Therefore, adopting a mindset of lifelong learning is not merely beneficial; it is essential for anyone involved in cybersecurity compliance.

To facilitate continuous learning, various resources are at your disposal. Webinars, workshops, and industry publications serve as invaluable tools in keeping pace with the latest trends and developments. These resources not only impart knowledge but also provide practical insights from experts actively working within the field. Engaging with such materials can help professionals develop a robust understanding of prevailing challenges and best practices in cybersecurity.

Webinars have become a cornerstone of ongoing education in cybersecurity. Organizations like the Cybersecurity and Infrastructure Security Agency (CISA) and the International Association of Privacy Professionals (IAPP) host regular webinars that delve into current issues ranging from threat detection techniques to compliance with new regulations like the California Consumer Privacy Act (CCPA). Participants benefit from real-time engagement with thought leaders, allowing them to ask questions and seek clarification on topics pertinent to their roles.

Workshops, too, play an essential role in fostering a deeper understanding of complex subjects. These interactive sessions allow participants to engage in hands-on learning experiences, translating theory into practice. For instance, a workshop focusing on incident response can provide participants with practical exercises that simulate real-world scenarios. This experiential learning is vital for developing skills that can be directly applied to workplace situations. Moreover, workshops often facilitate networking opportunities, connecting professionals who can share their experiences and insights, creating a community of forward-thinking guardians of the digital realm.

Industry publications are another crucial resource for continuous learning. Organizations like SANS, ISACA, and (ISC)^2 produce a wealth of materials, including whitepapers, research reports, and newsletters, that analyze the latest trends in cybersecurity. These publications often highlight case studies detailing the successes and failures of various organizations, providing readers valuable lessons about what works and what doesn't in the realm of compliance. Regularly engaging with these materials will not only keep you informed but also inspire you to think critically about your own cybersecurity practices.

Another platform worth exploring is online learning platforms, which offer a vast array of courses focusing on different aspects of cybersecurity compliance. Websites like Coursera, Udemy, and Pluralsight provide courses ranging from introductory topics to advanced techniques in threat analysis and risk management. These platforms often feature content created by industry experts, allowing learners to benefit from practical knowledge gleaned from years of experience. As a bonus, many of these courses are self-paced, making it easier for busy professionals to fit them into their schedules.

Furthermore, participation in cybersecurity conferences can significantly enhance your knowledge base and professional network. Events like the RSA Conference, Black Hat, and DefCon bring together practitioners, researchers, and thought leaders from across the globe. Attendees have the opportunity to hear keynote speeches from cybersecurity luminaries and participate in breakout sessions that cover cutting-edge topics. Engaging with peers during networking sessions fosters collaborations and discussions that can deepen one's understanding of compliance challenges and solutions.

As you dive into continuous education, it is crucial to recognize that effective learning occurs when you connect new information with existing knowledge. Reflect on your personal experiences in cybersecurity compliance and consider how the concepts presented in webinars or courses can be applied to your organization. The act of synthesizing new information with your personal insights not only reinforces learning but also empowers you to contribute to the development of your organization's cybersecurity strategy.

Personal reflections from industry experts can often serve as powerful motivators on your journey of continuous learning. Many leaders in cybersecurity compliance have faced similar challenges and obstacles. Their stories of triumph and failure can inspire you to embrace a culture of ongoing education. For instance, consider the journey of a compliance officer who faced the daunting task of aligning their organization with GDPR standards. Through relentless learning and adaptation, they transformed their approach to compliance, ultimately leading their organization to become a benchmark for others. Stories like these exemplify the potential rewards of dedicating time and resources to personal and organizational growth.

It is also important to highlight that a commitment to continuous learning extends beyond individual professional development. It should become a cornerstone of your organization's culture. Leadership plays a pivotal role in fostering this culture by promoting the value of ongoing education and establishing support systems that encourage employees to pursue learning opportunities. By integrating continuous learning into the fabric of your organization, you enhance the overall security posture and compliance sophistication of your business.

When organizational learning is prioritized, it creates an empowered workforce equipped with the latest knowledge and skills to tackle emerging threats and compliance challenges. Teams that engage in ongoing education are better prepared to respond proactively to incidents and adapt to changing regulatory environments. Leaders who champion this approach exemplify the innovative mindsets necessary for navigating the complexities of the digital realm.

In practice, implementing a continuous learning strategy can take various forms. Organizations might create learning programs that align with established professional development goals or incorporate learning objectives into performance reviews. Incentivizing participation in workshops and training sessions also demonstrates a commitment to employee growth and can lead to increased job satisfaction and retention.

Moreover, creating a knowledge base within the organization—whether through a centralized digital repository or regular knowledge-sharing meetings—can encourage staff to contribute to and benefit from cumulative learning. Providing access to recorded webinars, whitepapers, and course materials ensures that employees can engage with relevant content at their convenience.

Another strategic approach for reinforcing continuous learning is collaborating with external partners and educational institutions. Establishing partnerships with community colleges, universities, or industry associations can lead to collaborative programs that share resources and expertise. This not only enhances the learning opportunities available to employees but also fosters a sense of community and commitment to the broader cybersecurity landscape.

As the cybersecurity landscape continues to change, a commitment to staying informed is no longer optional; it is imperative. Developing a mindset of lifelong learning allows organizations and individuals to remain agile, adaptive, and resilient in the face of evolving threats and compliance requirements. By leveraging various resources such as webinars, workshops, and industry publications, cybersecurity professionals can keep pace with the latest developments and hone their skills.

Engaging with industry experts and reflecting on their learning journeys can inspire continuous growth and improvement, demonstrating that even seasoned professionals can benefit from ongoing education and learning. Furthermore, cultivating a culture of learning within organizations not only enhances individual skills but also strengthens collective cybersecurity efforts. Organizations that prioritize continuous education position themselves as leaders in compliance and security, fostering environments where innovation and adaptation thrive.

In conclusion, embracing continuous learning is the key to successfully navigating the complexities of cybersecurity compliance. Through proactive engagement with available resources and a commitment to cultivating a culture of education within their organizations, professionals can navigate the challenges of an ever-evolving landscape. The future of cybersecurity hinges upon our capacity to adapt, learn, and evolve in tandem with new threats and regulatory demands. By doing so, we can safeguard not only our organizations but also the broader digital ecosystem.

Chapter 11: Your Journey Towards Compliance

Celebrating Progress and Achievements

In the turbulent landscape of cybersecurity compliance, where the stakes are high and the threats ever-evolving, one aspect often overlooked is the importance of recognizing and celebrating progress. Organizations frequently become so entangled in addressing compliance requirements and mitigating risks that they neglect to acknowledge the milestones achieved along the way. Yet, this act of recognition is crucial, not just for morale, but for establishing a sustainable culture of accountability and commitment to ongoing cybersecurity efforts.

Celebrating achievements should be seen not merely as a formality; it is a strategy that reinforces the ethos within an organization that compliance is a continuous journey and not a mere checkbox exercise. By fostering an environment where milestones are celebrated, organizations cultivate resilience, innovation, and deeper engagement among their teams. This subchapter aims to explore the significance of recognizing achievements, provide effective strategies for measuring progress, and share inspiring stories of organizations that have embraced this practice.

The Importance of Recognition in the Compliance Journey

Recognition serves multiple purposes in the compliance journey. It reinforces positive behavior, provides motivation, and generates a sense of collective achievement among team members. When employees feel their hard work is appreciated, they are often more engaged and willing to take ownership of their roles in the compliance process. Celebrating milestones reflects the organization's commitment to transparency and growth. This celebration establishes accountability at every level, ensuring that compliance is viewed as an integral component of organizational culture.

Moreover, recognizing achievements can ease the pressure often associated with compliance. The cybersecurity landscape can be daunting, characterized by a complex web of regulations and standards that demand constant vigilance and adaptation. Celebrations serve as reminders that progress is not only possible but also being made. Whether a small win, such as passing an internal audit, or a major achievement, such as achieving certification under a recognized cybersecurity framework, these moments of celebration can significantly impact team morale.

Strategies for Measuring Progress

To celebrate progress effectively, organizations must first establish measurable indicators that allow them to track their compliance journey. These indicators provide a tangible way to assess milestones, progress, and challenges. Here are several effective strategies for measuring compliance progress:

1. Define Clear Objectives and KPIs: The foundation of any successful compliance journey is a clear understanding of objectives. Key Performance Indicators (KPIs) should be established for each aspect of compliance. Whether it's the percentage of completed training programs, the frequency of audits, or the reduction in security incidents, these measurable targets can help organizations gauge their compliance status effectively.

2. Regular Compliance Audits and Reviews: Conducting regular audits allows organizations to assess their adherence to compliance standards systematically. These audits can be internal or external and should focus on both the effectiveness of controls and compliance with regulations. After each audit, celebrate the successful findings and address the areas requiring improvement. For example, when an organization successfully navigates a rigorous compliance audit with few discrepancies, acknowledging this achievement fosters motivation for subsequent audits.

3. Progress Reports and Dashboards: Using dashboards or progress reports allows organizations to visualize their compliance journey. These tools can provide real-time insights into compliance status, such as the completion rates of employee training or the remediation of identified vulnerabilities. Sharing these reports with stakeholders creates transparency while recognizing collective achievements.

4. Feedback Mechanisms: Constant feedback from employees involved in compliance initiatives can provide valuable insights into what is working and what needs improvement. Conducting surveys or one-on-one discussions can facilitate open communication and

encourage team members to highlight their achievements and challenges. Recognizing an individual's contributions based on this feedback creates a culture of collaboration.

5. Celebrate Milestones: Much like project management methodologies that emphasize the need to recognize phases of a project, compliance journeys can benefit from recognizing milestones. Celebrating the completion of significant compliance stages, such as achieving national or international certification, can act as a rallying point for the entire organization.

Incorporating Celebrations into the Compliance Culture

Once organizations establish measurable indicators and progress, it's essential to create formal and informal celebrations. Here are some strategies organizations can implement to celebrate successes effectively:

1. Recognition Programs: Design formal recognition programs that highlight employees' contributions to compliance initiatives. This can include awards, shout-outs in meetings, or recognition in company communications. Consider implementing a “Compliance Champion” initiative, where team members are recognized for their efforts in advancing compliance.

2. Team Celebrations and Events: Host team events or gatherings to celebrate significant milestones. This could be a simple team lunch or an elaborate celebration event, depending on the importance of the achievement. These gatherings allow team members to share their experiences

and successes while reinforcing collective ownership of compliance efforts.

3. Storytelling: Emphasizing storytelling as a method to celebrate achievements can create a strong narrative around compliance journeys. Recognizing specific individuals or teams that overcame challenges can inspire others to adopt similar resilience. By sharing these stories in company newsletters or on internal communication platforms, organizations weave a narrative of triumph, reinforcing the importance of a collaborative compliance culture.

4. Engagement in Social Responsibility: Organizations can highlight compliance achievements by engaging in corporate social responsibility (CSR) initiatives. For example, if a company achieves compliance under specific data protection laws, it might decide to host a community event focusing on cybersecurity awareness. This creates a broader context for their compliance efforts and illustrates a commitment to protecting stakeholders beyond corporate walls.

Inspiring Stories of Successful Compliance Journeys

Moving beyond strategies, let's examine compelling stories of organizations that have successfully navigated their compliance journeys while embracing the importance of celebrating milestones. Each of these stories serves not just as examples of effective compliance but also as sources of inspiration for organizations at various stages in their own journeys.

Case Study 1: A Healthcare Provider Achieves HIPAA Compliance

A regional healthcare provider struggled with ensuring compliance with HIPAA regulations amidst challenges posed by data handling, patient privacy, and security threats. The organization refined its compliance processes by defining clear objectives, collaborating closely with a compliance officer, and investing in regular training programs for all employees.

After a challenging year of audits and improvements, the organization celebrated its successful HIPAA compliance certification. To mark this achievement, the leadership organized a company-wide event, highlighting the hard work of individual employees and departments that contributed to this success. In a heartfelt address, the CEO acknowledged the team's resilience while emphasizing the importance of maintaining compliance as an ongoing endeavor. This celebration fortified the organization's culture of compliance and encouraged teams to strive continuously for excellence.

Case Study 2: A Financial Institution's GDPR Journey

A financial institution faced immense pressure to comply with GDPR regulations. Understanding the significance of this legislation, executives rallied their teams and established a dedicated GDPR compliance working group, which involved members from various departments, including IT, marketing, and legal.

After two years of hard work, the institution successfully demonstrated its full compliance ahead of the implementation deadline. In celebration, they organized a company-wide

"GDPR Day," complete with discussions featuring key stakeholders who contributed to the compliance journey. The day included workshops on data privacy for employees, emphasizing an ongoing commitment to comply with regulatory changes. By publicly recognizing employees' hard work and celebrating their achievements, the organization fostered a culture of accountability, ensuring compliance remains everyone's responsibility.

Case Study 3: Engaging Employees at a Large Tech Firm

A large tech firm routinely found itself grappling with new cybersecurity regulations and standards. Leadership recognized that continuous learning and employee involvement were vital to their compliance strategy. They implemented regular training programs and opened channels for employee feedback.

Over time, the organization began to achieve significant milestones in its compliance journey. To celebrate these achievements, the company initiated a monthly "Compliance Spotlight," where different teams shared their best practices, success stories, and lessons learned, fostering a sense of community. Employees were eager to participate and recognize one another's contributions, transforming compliance into a platform for growth and learning.

These stories highlight that while compliance can feel like an uphill battle, celebrating milestones fosters a shared commitment and resilience.

Reflecting on the Compliance Journey

As organizations embark on their compliance journeys, it's critical to maintain a perspective that honors both individual and collective efforts. The significance of recognizing milestones cannot be overstated. Celebrations provide motivation, context, and a sense of purpose to compliance processes, allowing organizations to cultivate a continuous culture of accountability.

As you measure progress and establish recognition practices, remember that compliance is not merely about ticking off regulations—it's about nurturing a resilient, engaged, and informed workforce committed to protecting sensitive data and upholding ethical standards.

To empower teams, create a culture where progress is celebrated and excellence is pursued. Understand that each milestone, whether small or significant, deserves acknowledgment. By nurturing an environment where achievements are recognized and celebrated, organizations fortify their cybersecurity posture while continuing on the path of compliance. As the landscape of cybersecurity compliance evolves and new challenges arise, paying homage to the achievements of today will ensure a stronger foundation for the compliance endeavors of tomorrow.

With each celebration, organizations weave a narrative of commitment and resilience, ensuring that they are not only striving for compliance but are empowered in their collective journey towards securing the digital realm for all stakeholders involved.

Integrating Lessons Learned into Future Strategies

As organizations navigate the complex terrain of cybersecurity compliance, the ability to learn from past experiences and integrate these lessons into future strategies becomes crucial for sustained success. This journey is not linear; rather, it is an evolving process characterized by reflection, adaptation, and the continuous pursuit of improvement. In this subchapter, readers will discover approaches for integrating lessons learned into future compliance strategies, supported by real-world success stories that highlight the resilience and adaptability required in today's dynamic digital landscape.

One of the fundamental tenets of successful compliance is the commitment to reflection. Organizations must regularly take stock of their compliance efforts to understand what is working and what needs to be adjusted. Reflection provides an opportunity for teams to analyze historical performance, assess control effectiveness, and identify vulnerabilities that may have emerged over time. This practice of self-assessment creates a culture of accountability while setting a foundation for iterative improvement.

To begin the process of integrating lessons learned, organizations should establish a structured post-compliance review process. This initiative may arise after significant compliance milestones, such as achieving regulatory certification or completing an audit. By facilitating a comprehensive review session, organizations allow stakeholders to share insights and experiences, fostering an open dialogue about compliance successes and challenges faced throughout the process.

Consider the example of Techwise Solutions, a mid-sized technology company focused on data management. After successfully achieving compliance with the General Data Protection Regulation (GDPR), the organization conducted a post-compliance review to discuss the lessons learned during the rigorous process. Team members from various departments, including IT, legal, and operations, were invited to participate in this review, encouraging diverse perspectives and collective ownership of compliance. Through this collaborative effort, Techwise Solutions uncovered gaps in their employee training program, particularly in areas related to data privacy protocols.

Armed with this valuable insight, Techwise Solutions modified its training curriculum, incorporating real-world scenarios and role-playing exercises that highlighted potential compliance pitfalls. This curriculum change not only enhanced employee awareness but also created a more interactive and engaging learning environment. By reflecting on their past experiences, the company created a more robust and adaptable compliance strategy for the future.

Another key element of integrating lessons learned into future strategies is the willingness to adapt. The landscape of cybersecurity compliance is not static; it is subject to constant evolution driven by changes in technology, regulations, and threats. Organizations must remain agile and responsive to these changes, adjusting their compliance strategies accordingly.

One powerful mechanism for fostering adaptability is scenario planning. This strategic approach encourages organizations to envision different future scenarios based on emerging trends, such as increased data regulation or shifts in the threat landscape. By examining potential impacts and crafting response plans, organizations can better prepare for unforeseen events. In doing so, they not only enhance their compliance posture but also cultivate a mindset of proactive risk management.

For instance, GlobalFinance, a multinational corporation managing sensitive client data across multiple jurisdictions, employed scenario planning after identifying compliance gaps in its multi-region operations. Through a series of workshops facilitated by subject matter experts, the organization developed various hypothetical scenarios that addressed potential regulatory changes and emerging cyber threats. The team identified specific steps they would need to take for each scenario, ensuring they would remain compliant no matter the circumstances.

In the months following the scenario workshops, GlobalFinance observed changes in regulations impacting data transfer protocols, precisely as predicted. Thanks to their preparedness, the organization was able to swiftly align its operations with new compliance requirements—an achievement credited to their commitment to integration and flexibility.

Incorporating feedback loops into compliance processes is another vital component of integrating lessons learned. By establishing mechanisms for continuous feedback from employees, customers, and other stakeholders, organizations can gain insights into the effectiveness of their compliance initiatives. These feedback loops serve as a valuable source of information that can inform adjustments to training programs, policies, and procedures.

Consider the experience of HealthSecure, a healthcare organization with a strong emphasis on patient data protection. After completing a rigorous HIPAA compliance audit, they initiated a feedback process that involved engaging employees through anonymous surveys. The feedback collected from these surveys provided HealthSecure with quantifiable insights into the efficacy of their compliance training and overall data management practices. Employees expressed concerns about the complexity of the current procedures, prompting HealthSecure to streamline processes and provide additional resources to aid understanding.

Through this iterative feedback mechanism, HealthSecure created a culture of open communication that empowered employees to voice concerns and suggestions continuously. This approach not only improved compliance practices but also reinforced employee commitment to safeguarding patient data.

As organizations reflect on lessons learned and adapt strategies, it is essential to prioritize documentation and knowledge management. Establishing comprehensive documentation of compliance milestones, challenges, and successes creates a repository that can be referenced by current and future team members. This documentation should include a narrative of the organization's compliance journey, as well as best practices and insights that emerged during the process.

For example, a financial services firm, SecureBank, maintained detailed records throughout its journey toward compliance with the Payment Card Industry Data Security Standard (PCI DSS). By documenting the steps they took to enhance payment security and identify compliance gaps, SecureBank created a valuable knowledge base that became a reference point for onboarding new team members and updating existing policies.

Moreover, this documentation enabled SecureBank to engage in regular audits and serve as a foundation for continuous improvement. When the maintenance phase of compliance became necessary, the documentation allowed SecureBank to pinpoint areas that required additional attention and resources. As a result, the organization maintained its compliant status while cultivating a culture of knowledge sharing.

In addition to documentation, establishing clear performance metrics is essential for evaluating the effectiveness of compliance strategies. Organizations should define key performance indicators (KPIs) that align with their compliance goals. These KPIs can include metrics such as employee training completion rates, audit results, and incident response times. By tracking performance against these metrics, organizations can quantify their compliance journeys and identify specific areas for improvement.

An illustrative example can be drawn from the nonprofit sector, where ComplianceAid—a charity organization focused on protecting donor data—implemented performance metrics after its initial compliance with the Federal Information Security Management Act (FISMA). By monitoring KPIs such as data breach incidents and staff training participation rates, ComplianceAid was able to highlight the efficacy of its compliance initiatives and address any issues proactively.

As ComplianceAid progressed, the data revealed trends in employee training that indicated a need for enhanced interactivity within training sessions. With this data in hand, leadership adapted their training approach by incorporating gamification and real-life case studies, increasing engagement and retention among staff.

Finally, collaboration across departments is key to effectively integrating lessons learned into future compliance strategies. Compliance cannot exist in isolation; it must be a shared objective embraced by the entire organization. Establishing cross-departmental committees or task forces dedicated to exploring compliance-related challenges and solutions can facilitate knowledge sharing and innovative thinking.

For instance, an aerospace manufacturer, AeroTech, formed a cross-functional compliance committee comprising members from engineering, legal, IT, and operations. This committee was tasked with addressing compliance challenges related to export regulations and national security measures. By leveraging the expertise of diverse team members, AeroTech developed innovative solutions that harmonized compliance with operational efficiency.

The committee's collaborative approach led to the creation of a comprehensive compliance strategy that integrated regulatory adherence with business objectives. As a result, AeroTech not only ensured compliance but also gained a competitive advantage by streamlining operations and optimizing supply chain management.

As organizations continue to evolve their compliance strategies, it is important to remember that every lesson learned presents an opportunity for growth. Through intentional reflection, adaptation, feedback loops, robust documentation, performance metrics, and cross-departmental collaboration, organizations can navigate the cycles of compliance with confidence and resilience.

The path to effective compliance may be fraught with challenges, but those who embrace a journey of continuous improvement will position themselves for long-term success. The ability to learn from both triumphs and setbacks empowers organizations to remain agile in the face of evolving regulations and emerging threats.

In conclusion, integrating lessons learned into future compliance strategies is a dynamic process that requires commitment, introspection, and collaboration. As organizations adapt their strategies based on past experiences, they reinforce the understanding that compliance is not merely a one-time achievement but an ongoing journey—a journey vital to safeguarding sensitive data and maintaining the trust of stakeholders. By cultivating a culture of learning and adaptability, organizations can emerge as resilient guardians of the digital realm, prepared to navigate the complexities of cybersecurity compliance with confidence and foresight.

Empowering the Next Generation of Cyber Guardians

In a world where digital threats continuously evolve, the need for a strong, skilled workforce in cybersecurity has never been more urgent. The demand for professionals equipped to navigate the complexities of cybersecurity compliance and threat mitigation is reaching unprecedented heights. It is a responsibility not only of organizations to equip themselves but also of current professionals to mentor and empower the next generation of cyber guardians. The essence of this endeavor lies in recognizing that knowledge transfer, collaboration, and encouragement within the cybersecurity community will shape a resilient and adaptive future.

As we embark on this journey to empower the next generation, consider the vast tapestry of skills, experiences, and innovations that characterize the cybersecurity field today. Every seasoned professional has a unique narrative filled with lessons learned from both triumphs and failures. The act of sharing these narratives is crucial; it fosters a culture of learning, facilitating the agility that future guardians of the digital realm will need to succeed. Understanding the intricacies of compliance, threat response, ethical considerations, and technological advancements is fundamental, yet it is equally essential for new and aspiring cybersecurity professionals to learn from real-world experiences.

Mentorship serves as a bridge between experience and enthusiasm, connecting established professionals with newcomers eager to make their mark. A mentorship initiative rooted in transparency can transform the landscape of cybersecurity education and practice. Senior cybersecurity professionals oftentimes embody a wealth of knowledge accumulated through years of navigating the challenges of compliance, data security, incident response, and other critical areas. By sharing stories about strategies that worked, pitfalls that were encountered, and innovative solutions that were birthed from necessity, established professionals can profoundly impact the development of newcomers.

Initiating mentorship programs can take many forms. Organizations may establish formal mentorship pathways where junior employees are paired with seasoned cyber professionals. Alternatively, communities can create informal networking events where individuals share challenges they've faced within the realm of compliance and security. These gatherings serve as an incubator for nurturing relationships and stimulating discussions, allowing budding professionals to ask pressing questions that will ultimately guide their learning journeys.

To facilitate mentorship, it is important to cultivate a space where open communication thrives. Mentors should be encouraged to share resources that helped them along their journey, be it books, online courses, or invaluable industry contacts. These resources can support the professional growth of mentees, giving them essential tools to navigate their careers. Furthermore, mentors have the capacity to impart wisdom surrounding the realities of working in cybersecurity, including the importance of compliance and how it interplays with technical skills and individual accountability.

The role of mentorship doesn't rest only on the shoulders of seasoned professionals. As the landscape of cybersecurity diversifies and transforms rapidly, fresh perspectives from newer entrants to the field can also play a vital role. Those who have recently navigated educational systems, whether through formal traditional education or unconventional pathways like boot camps, possess a strong grasp of current trends and technologies. Their insights into the latest tools, methodologies, and industry shifts provide a valuable and dynamic exchange in the mentoring process.

Mentorship flourishes on the principle of reciprocity. While experienced professionals share their knowledge and insights, new professionals can also offer mentors fresh perspectives, innovative solutions, and updated knowledge of emerging technologies. This symbiotic relationship encourages continuous learning, enabling both parties to grow in their respective roles. As technologies evolve, mentorship can adapt—mentors may receive updates on the latest cybersecurity solutions, while mentees learn the importance of balancing legacy systems with innovative approaches.

In addition to formal mentorship relationships, communities should also embrace collaborative learning environments. Hackathons, workshops, and seminars offer platforms where cybersecurity enthusiasts can come together to solve problems, share insights, and innovate. These collaborative forums serve as creative breeding grounds, empowering individuals to take risks and experiment with their skills in a supportive environment. Facilitation of such activities is crucial for fostering an ecosystem of learning that transcends individual expertise.

Support for the next generation also extends beyond structured mentorship programs. The cybersecurity community must come together in its commitment to inclusion and diversity. A diverse workforce brings varied perspectives, which is especially beneficial in problem-solving and innovation. By encouraging underrepresented groups to pursue careers in cybersecurity and providing them with role models, organizations can enhance their resilience to evolving threats.

Educational institutions also have a significant role to play in nurturing the next generation of professionals. Curricula must reflect the demands of the industry by incorporating practical, hands-on experiences as well as opportunities for mentorship and guidance. Partnerships between educational institutions and organizations in the cybersecurity industry can provide students with real-world experiences. Internships, co-op programs, and job shadowing are essential for bridging the gap between education and industry requirements.

As professionals committed to nurturing the next generation of cyber guardians, we must advocate for accessibility to education and resources. The rise of online courses, webinars, and free resources has democratized cybersecurity education, making it increasingly attainable for individuals from all backgrounds. However, there is still much work to be done. Scholarship programs aimed at supporting underrepresented individuals in pursuing degrees or training in cybersecurity are vital. Prioritizing funding for such initiatives will empower individuals who might otherwise face barriers to joining the cybersecurity profession.

By engaging with educational institutions, organizations can also provide guest lectures, workshops, and participate in career days, fostering interest among students and guiding them toward successful career paths in cybersecurity. By nurturing a pipeline of new talent, the industry strengthens itself against the backdrop of mounting cyber threats.

Moreover, embracing lifelong learning is essential to staying relevant in the fast-paced world of cybersecurity. Encourage curiosity and a mindset of exploration in both mentors and mentees. Cybersecurity professionals must remain aware of evolving threats, new technologies, and shifting regulatory landscapes. Continuous education equips the workforce to adapt swiftly and remain effective in compliance efforts, compliance standards, and safeguarding digital assets.

In addition to mentoring and sharing knowledge, professionals should actively promote the importance of ethics in cybersecurity. Ethical considerations are paramount, as they shape a professional's approach to dealing with sensitive information, privacy, and compliance with regulations. Professionals must impart ethical guidelines as foundational principles, encouraging their mentees to view ethical decision-making as a compass guiding their actions in their careers. Discussing real-life ethical dilemmas can spark important conversations about integrity, accountability, and responsible decision-making.

The culture created through mentoring extends far beyond the roles of individual mentors and mentees. Establishing networks for cybersecurity professionals within industries allows individuals to exchange knowledge and best practices across sectors. Joining professional organizations such as the Information Systems Security Association (ISSA) or the International Association of Privacy Professionals (IAPP) enhances connectivity. By attending conferences and webinars, professionals in the field can network, seek guidance, and share experiences that will enrich the entirety of the cybersecurity landscape.

As the digital world becomes increasingly sophisticated, we must also recognize the pressures associated with working in cybersecurity—the emotional toll and the mental health implications of facing continuous threats. Mentoring relationships should prioritize mental health advocacy by enabling mentees to discuss challenges they might experience in their roles. A supportive network can provide coping mechanisms, stress management techniques, and wellness resources. Promoting mental wellness within the field cultivates a robust workforce prepared to confront evolving challenges.

To create a resilient community, we must practice proactive measures for knowledge sharing. Rather than waiting for challenges to arise, cybersecurity professionals should engage in sharing best practices related to compliance, threat detection, and risk management preemptively. Collaboration among professionals positions the industry to strengthen defenses and improve compliance standards continuously.

As individuals, we can amplify the impact of our mentoring efforts by actively seeking out opportunities to connect with younger generations outside of our direct professional circles. Engaging with communities through volunteerism, speaking at schools, or participating in local educational programs leverages our expertise to spark curiosity and passion for cybersecurity among young individuals. These interactions can plant the seeds that might grow into future careers, ensuring a robust cybersecurity community for years to come.

Empowering the next generation of cyber guardians transcends mere knowledge transfer; it fosters an ethos of collaboration, continuous learning, support, and ethical awareness. As we take on the mantle of mentorship, we contribute not only to the growth of individual professionals but also to the overall strength of the cybersecurity landscape. By investing in the future today, we create a legacy of resilience, adaptability, and innovation to combat the challenges that await us in the digital realm. Together, we can shape a proactive and prepared workforce, ensuring that the guardians of the digital realm are equipped to navigate the complexities and responsibilities of cybersecurity in an ever-evolving landscape.

In closing, we should take this moment to reflect on our role in shaping the future. Empowering the next generation involves not just teaching but listening; it means being open to feedback and fostering a culture of curiosity. The journey toward compliance and security is ongoing, and as experienced professionals in the cybersecurity arena, we have a responsibility to be proactive in guiding and nurturing the talent that will lead the charge against the cyber threats of tomorrow. By standing together, sharing our knowledge, and advocating for ethical practices, we will not only elevate individual careers but also fortify the collective strength of cybersecurity as a whole.

Conclusion

Dear Adventurers of the Cyber Realm,

What an exhilarating journey we've had! First off, I want to extend a huge THANK YOU for sticking with me and exploring the tumultuous yet fascinating seas of cybersecurity compliance! You've entered into the depths of knowledge, navigated promising pathways, and emerged ready to fortify your organization against lurking threats. This isn't just about pages filled with text and theories; together, we've illuminated strategies, uncovered pitfalls, and crafted actionable blueprints that will serve you well in your quest for cybersecurity mastery. I hope each chapter sparked your imagination and furnished you with a toolkit brimming with vibrant resources to tackle compliance effectively and confidently. From understanding the shadowy figures of cyber threats to securing the fortresses of governance, you've now got a treasure trove of insights at your fingertips! And let's be real—regardless of how advanced the technology gets, what remains constant is the crucial need for preparedness and knowledge. Embrace this mindset as you move forward; consider obstacles as stepping stones that strengthen your resolve and elevate the integrity of your organization. This book was crafted not just to inform, but to empower! You hold the tools, insights, and most importantly, the confidence to lead your organization into a safe and compliant future. I hope you feel invigorated and eager to apply everything you've learned! Remember, the cybersecurity landscape is a dynamic ecosystem, ever-changing and rife with opportunities for growth and advancement. Keep your curiosity alive and never stop learning! By doing so, you'll be poised to ride the waves of innovation while ensuring that compliance remains second nature. I wish you boundless success and hope you carry these lessons forth in your journey to safeguard not just your organization, but the digital realm at large. Together, let's promise to keep our spaces safe, secure, and thriving because every step we take towards compliance is a giant leap for digital security!

With all my gratitude,

Augustine E. Eta, Ph.D.

Made in the USA
Monee, IL
04 November 2026

67381212R00128